Stages of Power

REACTING CONSORTIUM PRESS

This book is a "reacting" game. Reacting games are interactive roleplaying games in which you, the student, are responsible for your own learning. They are used at more than 300 colleges and universities in the United States and abroad. Reacting Consortium Press is a publishing program of the Reacting Consortium, the association of schools that use reacting games. For more information visit http://reactingconsortiumpress.org.

Stages of Power

MARLOWE AND SHAKESPEARE, 1592

ERIC S. MALLIN AND
PAUL V. SULLIVAN

REACTING
CONSORTIUM PRESS

The University of North Carolina Press has been a
member of the Green Press Initiative since 2003.

ISBN 978-1-4696-3144-8 (pbk.: alk. paper)
ISBN 978-1-4696-3145-5 (ebook)

Cover illustration: *Queen Elizabeth going in procession to
Blackfriars in 1601*, attributed to Robert Peake the Elder, ca. 1600
(courtesy of Everett Collection Historical / Alamy Stock Photo).

Distributed by The
University of North Carolina Press
116 South Boundary Street
Chapel Hill, NC 27514-3808
1-800-848-6224
www.uncpress.unc.edu

Contents

Stages of Power

1

Introduction

This game enacts artistic, political, moral, and religious conflicts in England in the autumn of 1592. These conflicts play out in a contest between two rival acting companies for a license to perform one of two plays: Christopher Marlowe's *Tragical History of Doctor Faustus* (or another of his plays, as chosen by the game master) or William Shakespeare's *Richard III* (or one of his other early plays).

Christopher Marlowe is the most successful playwright in the city, and his acting company, the Lord Admiral's Men, is eager to stage one of his plays. The theaters have been closed since June because of an outbreak of bubonic plague. Actors are anxious about their livelihoods, and they want a winning script. The manager of the theater where the Lord Admiral's Men perform would ordinarily be happy to produce any Marlowe play, but some of his themes are potentially controversial, and City officials are skittish. They remember too well decades of violent collisions between Protestants and Catholics and continuing factional rivalries between noblemen and courtiers. Now there are new rumblings of Puritan[1] discontent and foreign meddling in affairs of state. There are even rumors that Marlowe is an atheist.

1. **Puritan:** According to the *Oxford English Dictionary*, this term first appeared in the 1560s. It originally meant "a member of a group of English Protestants of the late 16th and 17th centuries, who regarded the reformation of the Church under Elizabeth I as incomplete and sought to remove any remaining elements of church practice (such as ceremonies, church ornaments, the use of musical instruments, and in some cases episcopal authority) which they considered corrupt, idolatrous, or unscriptural." It took on a broader meaning, "A member of any religious group that advocates or aspires to special purity of doctrine or practice." Both meanings were current in the 1590s. In the world of this game, the Puritans are a problem, as they threaten to unsettle the so-called Elizabethan Settlement of Religion, a middle way between Catholic and radical Protestant doctrines and practices.

The Queen's master of the revels will not allow mere scribblers to threaten the fragile balance of public order. Might there be a safe and profitable alternative to Marlowe? A rival company, Lord Strange's Men, has had some success with the plays of a young actor named William Shakespeare, and he has a new script to offer now. Strange's Men are an able troupe, and they have performed the young poet's work to some acclaim. But will Marlowe's play survive official scrutiny in these nervous times? Perhaps more important, will it win audiences? While the theater manager waffles, the Queen's Privy Council has agreed to oversee a contest between the Lord Admiral's Men and Lord Strange's Men to decide which troupe will be licensed to reopen the playhouses. Which actors are better, and which play? Which will best represent the nation's ideals, energies, humor, and grandeur without overt offense to political or religious order?

The players have an impressive command of texts and traditions that inform Elizabethan struggles of religion, rank, and power, struggles that were moved by the dynamics of dramatic spectacle, eloquent speech, and ruthless scheming. In debate and in performance before the Privy Council, the rival companies play out the dramas of their age: lofty humanist ideals and poetic art take wing in the theater, only to be brought to earth by the pragmatic rhetoric of the City and the cynical, secretive maneuverings of the court and Privy Council. By the end of the game, one troupe will gain supremacy (fleeting though it may be) and win a license to play at the Rose Theatre, thereby increasing their fortunes.

HOW TO PLAY THIS GAME

This is a "reacting" game. Reacting games are historical role-playing games in which students take on assigned characters to learn about moments in history. After a few preparatory lectures, the game begins and the students are in charge. Set in moments of heightened historical tension, the games place students in the roles of historical figures. By reading the game book and their individ-

ual role sheets, students discover their objectives, potential allies, and the forces that stand between them and victory. They must then attempt to achieve victory through formal speeches, informal debate, negotiations, and (sometimes) conspiracy. Outcomes sometimes part from actual history; a postmortem session sets the record straight.

The following is an outline of what you will encounter in this game and what you will be expected to do.

Game Setup

Your instructor will spend some time before the beginning of the game helping you to understand its historical context. During the setup period, you will use several different kinds of material:

- The game book (from which you are reading now), which includes historical information, rules and elements of the game, and essential documents.
- A role sheet, provided by the instructor, which gives a short biography of the historical figure you will model in the game as well as that person's ideology, objectives, responsibilities, and resources. Your role may be an actual historical figure or a composite.

In addition to the game book, you may also be required to read historical documents or literary criticism. These provide additional information and arguments for use during the game.

Read all of this material and all of these documents and sources before the game begins. And, just as important, go back and reread these materials throughout the game. A second and third reading while *in role* will deepen your understanding and alter your perspective, for ideas take on a different aspect when seen through the eyes of a partisan actor.

Students who have carefully read the materials and who know the rules of the game will invariably do better than those who rely on general impressions and uncertain memories.

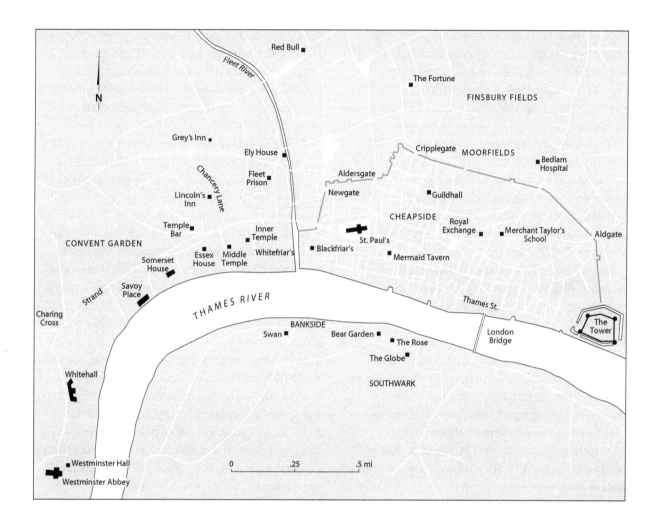

Game Play

Once the game begins, class sessions are presided over by students. In most cases, a single student serves as a kind of presiding officer. The instructor then becomes the game master (GM) and takes a seat in the back of the room. Though they do not lead the class sessions, GMs may do any of the following:

- Pass notes.
- Announce important events. Some of these events are the result of student actions; others are instigated by the GM.
- Redirect proceedings that have gone off track.

The GM is expected to observe basic standards of fairness, but as a fail-safe device, this game employs the "Podium Rule," which allows a student who has not been recognized to approach the podium and wait for a chance to speak. Once at the podium, the student has the floor and must be heard.

Role sheets contain private, secret information that students are expected to guard. You are advised, therefore, to exercise caution when discussing your role with others. Your role sheet probably identifies likely allies, but even they may not always be trustworthy. However, keeping your own counsel, or saying nothing to anyone, is not an option. In order to achieve your objectives, you *must* speak with others. You will never muster the voting strength to prevail without allies. Collaboration and coalition building are at the heart of every game.

These discussions must lead to action, which often means proposing, debating, and passing legislation or petitions of various kinds. Always remember that this game is *only a game*—resistance, attack, and betrayal are not to be taken personally, since game opponents are merely acting as their roles direct.

Some games feature strong alliances called *factions*; these are tight-knit groups with fixed objectives. Games with factions all include roles called Indeterminates. They operate outside the established factions. Not all Indeterminates are entirely neutral; some are biased on certain issues. If you are in a faction, cultivating Indeterminates is in your interest, since they can be convinced to support your position. If you are lucky enough to have drawn the role of an Indeterminate, you should be pleased; you will likely play a pivotal role in the outcome of the game.

Game Requirements

Players will practice persuasive writing, public speaking, critical thinking, teamwork, negotiation, problem solving, collaboration, adapting to changing circumstances, and working under pressure to meet deadlines. Your instructor will explain the specific requirements for your class. In general, though, this game asks you to perform three distinct activities:

Reading and Writing. This standard academic work is carried on more purposefully in a role-playing game, since what you read is put to immediate use, and what you write is meant to persuade others to act the way you want them to. The reading load may have slight variations from role to role; the writing requirement depends on your particular course. Papers are often policy statements, but they can also be autobiographies, battle plans, spy reports, newspapers, poems, or after-game reflections. Papers provide the foundation for the speeches delivered in class.

Public Speaking and Debate. In the course of a game, almost everyone is expected to deliver at least one formal speech from the podium (the length of the game and the size of the class will determine the number of speeches). Debate follows. Debate can be impromptu, raucous, and fast paced, and results in decisions voted on by the body. GMs may stipulate that students must deliver their papers from memory when at the podium, or may insist that students wean themselves from dependency on written notes as the game progresses.

Wherever the game imaginatively puts you, it will surely not put you in the classroom of a twenty-first-century American college. Accordingly, the colloquialisms and familiarities of today's college life are out of place. Never open your speech with a salutation like "Hi guys" when something like "Fellow citizens!" would be more appropriate.

Never be friendless when standing at the podium. Do your best to have at least one supporter second your proposal, come to your defense, or admonish inattentive members of the body. Note-passing and side conversations, while common occurrences, will likely spoil the effect of your speech, so you and your supporters should insist on order before such behavior becomes too disruptive. Ask the presiding officer to assist you, if necessary, and the GM as a last resort.

Strategizing. Communication among students is an essential feature of this game. You will find yourself writing e-mails, texting, attending out-of-class meetings, or gathering for meals on a fairly regular basis. The purpose of frequent communication is to lay out a strategy for advancing your agenda and thwarting the agenda of your opponents, and to hatch plots to ensnare individuals troubling to your cause. When communicating with a fellow student in or out of class, always assume that he or she is speaking to you in role. If you want to talk about the "real world," make that clear.

COUNTERFACTUALS

Troupes of actors would not have commingled with the Privy Council as they do in this game.

Essex was not named to the council until 1593, but we will imagine for the purposes of this game that he is already there, named to the chamber shortly after the younger Cecil in 1592.

2

Historical Background

1485: Henry Tudor defeats King Richard III in battle and becomes King Henry VII of England, ending decades of dynastic violence (the "War of the Roses") and founding the Tudor dynasty.

1509: Henry VIII succeeds his father as king, and marries Catherine of Aragon, his brother's widow. The young king is hailed as a model of the Christian monarch steeped in the New Learning.

1521: Henry VIII publishes a scholarly defense of papal supremacy against the claims of Protestant reformers. Pope Leo X rewards Henry with the title Defender of the Faith.

1527: Henry VIII seeks a divorce from Catherine, as he does not have a legitimate son. His efforts are blocked by the pope and by the Queen's nephew, the Holy Roman emperor.

1533: In January, Henry VIII marries Anne Boleyn, having declared his previous marriage to Catherine of Aragon null and void. He is excommunicated by the Roman Catholic Church.

1533: Anne Boleyn gives birth to a daughter, Elizabeth.

1534: Henry VIII declares himself head of the Church of England, breaking from the Roman Catholic Church.

1547: Henry VIII dies at Whitehall Palace. Edward VI, age ten, succeeds his father as king. During the boy king's brief reign, powerful noblemen and churchmen push the Church of England toward the more radical Protestantism of European reformers like John Calvin.

1548: The new Book of Common Prayer, embodying Protestant reforms, is made compulsory in Church of England practice.

1553: Edward VI dies and his sister Mary becomes Queen Mary I. She soon begins the restoration of the Roman Catholic Church in England and the violent persecution of Protestants that wins her the name "Bloody Mary."

1558: Mary I dies, and her sister becomes Queen Elizabeth I.

1559: The young queen soon begins the reform of the Church of England, making the English monarch supreme head of the church and making the use of a revised Book of Common Prayer compulsory. Over the course of her long reign, the church settles uneasily into a "via media," a middle way, amid official persecutions of Catholics and rising discontent from Puritan Protestants.

1564: In February, Christopher Marlowe is born in Canterbury, son of a shoemaker. In April, William Shakespeare is born in Stratford-upon-Avon, son of a glovemaker.

1569: Thomas Percy, Seventh Earl of Northumberland, leads the Northern Rebellion, aiming to depose Elizabeth I and put the Catholic Mary, Queen of Scots, on the throne. The Northern rebel leaders are defeated and flee to Scotland.

1570: Pope Pius V issues a declaration proclaiming Queen Elizabeth I a heretic and urging all English Catholics to disobey her.

1572: Up to 30,000 French Protestants are massacred by Catholics in a months-long event beginning on Saint Bartholomew's Day. This real-life horror story will be revived by Christopher Marlowe in a play for the London stage.

1576: James Burbage, actor, founds The Theatre in Shoreditch, the first public amphitheater in London since Roman times.

1577: Another open-air public theater, The Curtain, opens in Finsbury Fields, London.

1580: Sir Francis Drake returns in his ship, the *Golden Hind*, laden with spices and Spanish gold after circumnavigating the globe, a glorious triumph for England.

1586: The Queen's spymaster, Sir Francis Walsingham, discovers (after conniving to encourage the conspirators) the so-called Babington Plot to assassinate Elizabeth and put Mary Stuart (Mary, Queen of Scots) on the throne. Mary is tried and found guilty of treason.

1587: Elizabeth I signs a death warrant and Mary Stuart is executed at Fotheringhay.

1587: The Rose, the first theater on Bankside, just south of the Thames, opens.

1588: The English fleet defeats the Spanish Armada, a glorious victory for Elizabeth I and for Protestantism in England. Philip II, Catholic king of Spain, had launched the massive fleet to enforce by conquest his claim to the throne of England as his right by marriage to Queen Mary I.

1592: The bubonic plague breaks out in London. It will prove to be the most serious episode of the illness in England since 1563.

PROLOGUE

29 October 1592

My Dear Mall,
Late arrived on the edge of the city, and I have much to tell. Most, the heavy miss I have of thee! my good heart and true. My occasion for leaving was all for the best, though for sorrow the worst. Pray to God that we shall soon find each other again.

The travel was hard, the mare that cousin George loaned me spavined and slow, the food along the way very poor and the inn beds full of fleas. The sickness was near as bad in towns along the road as it was in Winchester when I left you, worse in some places. Not all the dead are even buried yet, and some streets seem like woodcuts carved from the Book of Revelation. But fear not for me, as my faith in God will provide and protect. Though dreadful sickness and the sinning multitude still live and reign in the city, and there's no safety anywhere in these parlous times, yet God's wrath seems to have abated somewhat—no one knows why. Signs of life return: the ships are once more being allowed into port; some shops open again, at least those whose proprietors have not died; and I hear some of the trades are hiring, although I have not seen't.

You think me mad, traveling into the late-infected city, but needs must. Mall, had I friends at court, or any gifts I could bring to the nobility, it might earn us a noble—I could find a patron. In the inn at Chertsey where I rested for a night I talked with a man who said a skilled scrivener might soon find work in London. For though the sickness has slowed the business of the court and the lawyers and the merchants of the City, it has also made places for new men by killing off the old ones. This fellow's father was like mine a hard-handed man, a carpenter of Guildford, but now this one is a King's Scholar and a proper popinjay in his Oxford gown. When we had drunk some he tried to best me in reciting Latin verses but I am even five years out of school the better scholar. I can bless Master Harmar for his teaching, though I still grumble in my heart at how he turned me out of my scholarship when pressed to make room for a rich man's son. In bitterness I ask, what has learning made me but a hireling scribbler, and little better than a masterless man? I pray God turn my crabbed heart away from proud and sinful thoughts of how I might have served Him as a minister of His faith with my good wife at my side in the business of a parish. "The race is not to the swift," saith the preacher. But luck may still come our way, and a better chance might present itself.

Coming into Southwark a fortnight ago I went straightway to Winchester Palace where Master Harmar now directs our bishop's great work of Englishing holy books from the Greek. I waited on him some three hours before he came out to me. He greeted me lovingly, but sorrowfully said he can give me no work now as the bishop supplies him clerks aplenty and money none. Yet he kindly directed me to decent lodgings

and cheap nearby. My landlord is sometime sexton of Saint Mary Overie Church, a merry man but honest I do think. He keeps a tavern in his house at the sign of the Elephant and here I take my meals when not across the bridge in the city seeking work. I pay but little here for the neighborhood is not of the best. Truth to tell, the leaping houses, bear-baiting pit, and playhouses are all hard by my lodgings, built here beyond the reach of the City's laws. Fear not sweet wife that I keep unwholesome company or forget my pledged troth, but trust that I am learning to make my way among the snares of the city. Indeed from one of the actors who drink at the Elephant I have found some small work copying plays as I shall tell thee anon. And even here on the south bank I hear much talk of great matters of state.

The city goes from one fear to the next, it seems, and our security lies far removed from us, along with proper order and general welfare. Streets overflow with beggars, some of them recently released prisoners from Fleet; but far more in number are the lame and the wounded soldiers from our many wars abroad and in Ireland. If the Queen ever calls another parliament, I know our burgess was planning to devise a bill "for the necessary relief of soldiers and mariners." But the hopeless rabble are scarce the only danger, as you know. The Q. her sacred majesty ages, it is not long since Catholics laid bugbears on her life, and with none to succeed her, and still no heir named, the situation gives hope to all sects who wish for supremacy. The city has found no peace from the wars of religion that so roiled the harmony of the world. A mad Puritan messiah, William Hackett, is remembered with scorn, who lost his life in a bloody, barbarous execution because he thought the Queen's middle way the wrong one; he proclaimed himself the child of God, braved the crowd wild for his quartering alive. And I have no doubt that should the royal men find

Martin Marprelate,[1] he will meet a similar end. Fortunate am I to profess what I believe, which happens to be the Queen's faith. The others have their followers, but have been driven underground. Word bruits about that another bill is planned to confine all Catholics within five miles of their residence and to prevent the more vehement Puritans from disobedience in word or deed. With the rise in prices and the scarcity of food because of the plague, no man counts his safety as sure. Today I heard that some men like the famous Doctor Simon Forman have in despair or just impatience with the disorder and the sickness turned to magic and necromancy. If prayer and medicines fail, we try what we may.

Mine own prayers have gone unanswered here these many days, and much have I been tested and tried. The purse empties, and the only offers I've received have been in the disreputable pockets of the City. I did not know such ill professions had names: turner, pitcher, cross biter, procurer. The others are not for your ears, dear heart! Yet perhaps I can return with some fortune, if all goes well. This morning I sought your uncle Ingram, who keeps his state at a tavern in Deptford near the house of his master, Thomas Walsingham. There I found uncle full of making merry with three fine gentles all full of news. Has word of the great ship flown homeward yet? I'll tell you: there are riches here aplenty, and indirectly I may gain from them. Even as I arrived, a frightful commotion was raised near the ports: Sir Walter Ralegh, the famous courtier, and his shipmen captured the immense Spanish carrack *Madre de Dios*, stole it, and brought it to harbor. I hear it is plundered without shame, but not by Ralegh.

1. **Marprelate:** In 1588 and 1589 a number of sensational pamphlets penned by "Martin Marprelate" (a pseudonym) circulated widely, attacking the governing bishops of the Church of England and sympathizing with the more radical Puritan position.

Common townsmen did swarm in and carry its store away, some hundred pounds at a time. Report gives out the Queen's displeasure was frightful. To prevent the theft, she has dispatched a small constabulary force led by Robert Cecil himself to try to arrest the thieves, and to recover some of her goods and guard the rest. (They are Spain's goods, but royalty makes no such nice distinctions.) Cecil has engaged Walsingham and he in turn good uncle Ingram to gather intelligence of the stolen goods and to make an inventory of what remains in the ship. A goodly portion has already slipped through the Queen's fingers, and found its way to the shops, the streets, and, I hear, even the playhouses. My uncle bade me come again tomorrow to the tavern in the house of Mrs. Bull at Deptford to write for him the inventory. He says there is a week's work and may be more copying after. He says as well he knows the best men among the actors, and that printers will pay well for copies of plays. Should I never profit from the plundering of the ship, at least it has given me conceit of a new direction for my labor. There at Mrs. Bull's house I shall see some of Ingram's friends and the good men of the theater, and though you doubt, I believe it may be the best hope for my skills, and our fortune.

The theater, though of ill repute in the country, has growing fame in the city, so much so that the Queen herself has become involved in its doings. Court performances have been suspended because Her Majesty decreed, in this still sick time, that none should approach within two miles of court who have no reason to attend on her (and all masterless men to be arrested). But there is much bustle among the companies anyway, returning from their shows abroad, and the Q. and her ministers prepare for the new public playing season, should the illness abate enough.

Much bashing of brains on the matter has come to this: some on the council and in

Parliament, who are friends of the Lord Mayor, think the playhouses should remain shuttered forever and that all such actors and their associates should be imprisoned or removed from London, as if they were the cause of the troubles here. But Her Majesty not only insists on opening the stages once more, but has approved a plan to see if the best men win. I mean, Master Tilney of the Revels Office and Master Coke the lawyer will oversee a competition, so the rumor has it, between the two great companies, Lord Strange's Men and the Lord Admiral's Men, before the Privy Council.

These troupes have the lion's share of fame in the city. Although detractors clip the wings of both, and the Puritans hate them rootedly, the crowds still flock to see them whatever they play. Why, it is told that Strange's Men have a "Seven Deadly Sins" show, lifted straight from those morality plays your father's grandfather acted in Coventry, and all sorts of foolery happens on stage—jigs immediately after the darkest tale of woe (usually the clown Kemp performs one of these for Strange, and the Admiral's Men have their own dancers, usually a fellow named Pope or that writer Munday).

From all that I hear the Admiral's Men are a bit more popular, for they have the great Ned Alleyn. But I will say that I have heard stories of Strange's Men's shows, and they have wild joy in their playing, and they put on bigger plays, with more characters and changes of scene. Strange's Men sometimes offer powerful slander on the stage, jest in public about the ill morals of their rivals; the Admiral's Men play the words of Marlowe, a poet who rarely speaks well of the powerful, to the great amusement of the many. Yet both troupes compete cheerfully, as if the world were their carnival.

Mall, what a life this would be, to join a troupe! Each has poets scribbling new plays as fast as they can, and there is always copying of parts for the actors. And the printers by Paul's church will pay a week's wage for a whole play. I shall find out whether they can use my talents, and beg good uncle Ingram's kindness to put in a good word with Marlowe's Company.

Best little magpie, I have more to tell thee, and will say what unfolds with the actors' contest. I believe the pestilence brings this cry of players to the Inns of Court, which is where Mr. Coke, newly named speaker of the House of Commons, will preside over the game (it is said that the Queen is watching from afar, and her spies are everywhere). Although attendance is forbid for any but the privileged, word may come down from Mrs. Bull, whom I hear has been invited to wait on the proceedings by none other than the Lord Secretary for whom she does good service now and then, says Uncle Ingram. I shall send you all news that I hear of the matter, for my fortunes may well ride on those of the winning troupe. Win or lose, I hope one shall have me.

So good my mouse I have no mo' news for thee, but that the writing of this letter has cheered me, which bodes well for my new profession, if I can manage it. And it bodes well for us, if I can secure hire-and-salary.

Remember me, faith, heartily, and also remember me to my brother Rob't and my father, and my mother in her infirmity. Though the sickness be near thee, let it escape our hearth and leave our village—which it shall, by the grace of God. Do not forget to follow the advice of Doctor Kellwaye, in keeping all things about the house clean and tidy, and throwing water before our door, and having good store of rue, rosemary, and other herbs in thy windows. Light the fires at night and say thy prayers and the Lord will mercifully defend thee. My best commendation to all our friends who yet live, family, and to thee my love. Please send word of my garden and the town, and brook my absence with patience. I go now to lodge near the theaters, and to think of thee every day and always.

Thy Loving Walter—
Wat

THE STORY TODAY

It is October 1592 in London. Christopher Marlowe, the most accomplished playwright in the city, has written a new work, *The Massacre at Paris*, which his company, the Lord Admiral's Men, is understandably eager to read and rehearse. That's because the usually lucrative theater season has been postponed since June. The bubonic plague has been spied in outlying parishes, and the Privy Council has recently enforced the statute stipulating that the theaters must close when plague deaths in the city reach thirty per week. Theaters have been closed from the end of June to the beginning of Michaelmas term (September 29); the actors and theater employees are anxious about their finances, and they had better come up with a good play to perform. The acting companies are nervous about the upcoming season. Repertory rehearsals have not gone well, as several actors fled the diseased city to tour the provinces, but spent most of their time drinking; they are out of practice, have forgotten their parts, and are only now returning to London.

Philip Henslowe, the manager of the Rose Theatre, where the Lord Admiral's Men perform, would ordinarily be happy to debut Marlowe's new script, but the subject—the Saint Bartholomew's Day Massacre—is neither pleasant nor neutral, and the play's strongly anti-Catholic stance might inflame hostilities against suspected Catholics and recusant sympathizers, such as some foreign merchants on whom so much of London's trade depends. Henslowe knows that the Lord Mayor and the City aldermen might be pleased with the anti-Papist sentiment but will revile the prospect of civic disorder. And he can never quite keep these religious controversies straight. He needs to play it safe, especially in this dicey season.

Should he simply return to the most popular play from last year—Marlowe's *The Jew of Malta*? Or perhaps he should insist on another proven play of Marlowe's, *The Tragical History of Doctor Faustus*. Though the story, about a German magician, has anti-Catholic elements, it could provide audiences with excitement and novelty without the incendiary risks of the play about Saint Bartholomew's Day.

Rumors of Marlowe's atheism, however, have begun to make waves among London City authorities. Furthermore, Edmund Tilney, master of the Queen's revels (and the chief censor of the realm), has come under scrutiny from the Privy Council of late; they have been urging him to particular vigilance over any triggers of disorder that he might spot in the theater: seditious, heretical, or "precisian" (Puritan) tendencies in the playhouses. Tilney certainly does not need an acting company— one that cares mainly about profit—getting him into trouble over matters of religion or state. The actors thus need an alternative play to ensure a profitable but secure return to playing; Tilney needs to be sure that such a play cannot be considered a threat to public order, or he will have to fine the companies and possibly close down the theaters.

A relatively new but accomplished company, Lord Strange's Men, boasts a young, somewhat successful writer named William Shakespeare, who is said to have several barnburners in the queue. Strange's Men are a good group, and have performed many times, and well, at the Rose before. Even Ned Alleyn, the Lord Admiral's great actor, has sometimes played with them while between jobs. A vital theater season can mean big profits, even for the master of the revels, and as time passes and the actors languish, Tilney grows more anxious. Last night, after two cups of wine, he decided to contact both companies with bold offers to license their plays and get the profits rolling in.

But this morning all plans are off. Disaster. A letter from the Privy Council. Some busybody on the council (probably under the influence of the killjoy Puritans in the city) has thrown up an obstacle they have used before. Too well Tilney remembers a similar letter he received in November 1589 (as the Privy Council records show):

A letter to the Master of the Revelles requiring him [to join] with two others the one to be appointed by the Lord Archbishop of Canterbury and the other by the Lord Mayour of London, to be men of learning and judgement, and to call before them the severall companies of players (whose servauntes soever they be) and to require them by authorite hereof to delyver unto them their bookes, that they maye consider of the matters of their comedyes and tragedyes, and thereupon to stryke oute or reforme suche partes and matters as they shall fynd unfytt and undecent to be handled in playes, bothe for Divinitie and State, comaunding the said companies of players, in her Majesties name, that they forbeare to present and playe publickly anie comedy or tragedy other then suche as they three shall have seene and allowed, which if they shall not observe, they shall then knowe from their Lordships that they shalbe not onlely sevearely punished, but made incapable of the exercies of their profession forever hereafter.[1]

That commission of three sniped and quibbled on and on, while actors (and Tilney's purse) grew lean. This new commission promises to be even worse: the council has appointed six (six!) ambitious men who are even less likely to be able to agree among themselves. Including Tilney, we have the Archbishop of Canterbury, that eager persecutor of Puritans and Catholics; the firebrand Earl of Essex; his nemesis the bustling bureaucrat Sir Robert Cecil; the Queen's omnipresent treasurer Lord Burghley (who just happens to be Cecil's father); and Edward Coke, the Queen's hawkeyed lawyer. Everyone knows that factional hatreds run deep among these men. The Queen even seems to encourage their squabbling.

And the council has deputized Tilney—O woe to him!—to lead the proceedings. Though the

lowest in rank, he has extensive experience with this unglamorous occupation, the theater. The commission will ask for arguments and see rehearsals from both troupes. They will of course be on the lookout for matters of sedition and irregularity, but they also have been given to understand that expressive latitude must be allowed: the Queen enjoys the private performances she has received from the London companies over the years, she is happy to have the troupes under the protection of her nobility against the statutes forbidding vagabonds, and she would frown upon the restraint of their trade for any but the most urgent causes.

Which troupe is better? Who will most effectively represent the nation's ideals and spirit, humor and grandeur? In the past, Lord Strange's Men have proven to be (at least, to Tilney and to the Privy Council) somewhat more trouble than the Lord Admiral's, as theater historian Lawrence Manley observes:

In the study of Elizabethan acting companies and their repertories, Strange's Men must loom large. An older company reinvigorated by actors taken from other companies in the late 1580s . . . [and modeled] on the Queen's Men, a company formed in 1583, Strange's was a large-scale company whose ambitious and daring productions quickly surpassed those of the Queen's Men in popularity. . . .

Performing under the patronage of an inscrutable nobleman who was said to be "of all three religions and . . . of none," the company appears to have courted controversy by being unusually defiant of authority. In November 1589, at the height of the Marprelate controversy, the Lord Mayor of London complained to Burghley that when he instructed "the L. Admeralles and the L. Straunge's players . . . to forbere playinge, . . . the L. Admeralles players very dutifullie obeyed, but the others in very Contemptuous manner departing from me, went to the Crosse keys and played that after-

1. Minutes of the Privy Council, November 12, 1589, in *The Elizabethan Stage*, vol. 4, ed. E. K. Chambers (Oxford: Clarendon, 1951), 306–7.

noon, to the greate offence of the better sorte that knewe they were prohibited by order." . . . In February 1592, when Strange's Men opened at the Rose, they appear to have staged their second performance on a Sunday; they did not immediately repeat the practice, but the Lord Mayor of London shortly afterward began corresponding with Archbishop Whitgift about suppressing the playhouses because they were drawing apprentices and servants "from sermons & other Christian exercises."[1]

Truthfully, all actors and troupes were problematic, and so there were numerous ways to restrain them: religious strictures, civic orders, monarchical decrees. The Queen trusts Tilney to regulate the stage, and relies on her council, but she always includes a backup mechanism. Therefore, the great jurist Edward Coke will act as Her Majesty's silent observer and informant. She would observe the proceedings herself, but for the highly disreputable fame of the acting professions and their environs, described here by Jessica A. Browner:

> It is hardly surprising that the area in and around Southwark became the main center of dissipation of sixteenth- and seventeenth-century London. In its range of purveying (with all its shades of meaning) and social and communal functions, it had its own existence within and yet separate from established society. Added to this, however, was a more defined jurisdictional distinction: it was a place where the Mayor's writ, if not always the King's, did not run. Those who had no place in the paternal hierarchy of society—the "masterless" men—came here, bringing with them the alleged baggage of crime and sedition. The expansive apprentice population made it a traditional place of disorder, especially when political protest was incited; even its topography seems to have encouraged it. Combine with this the number and, indeed, supposed increase in the number of degenerate establishments—from bowling alleys to brothels to baiting rings—and Southwark's disreputable reputation was assured.[1]

The extraordinary occasion of the game therefore posits contact between some of the most powerful and least powerful persons of the realm. Both groups will find their fortunes altered, perhaps considerably, by the events of the next few weeks.

1. Lawrence Manley, "From Strange's Men to Pembroke's Men: 2 *Henry VI* and *The First part of the Contention*," *Shakespeare Quarterly* 54, no. 3 (2003): 253–87; 254.

1. Jessica A. Browner, "Wrong Side of the River: London's Disreputable South Bank in the Sixteenth and Seventeenth Century," *Essays in History* 36 (1994): 72.

3

The Game

MAJOR ISSUES FOR DEBATE

Two acting companies will compete to persuade the Privy Council to grant an exclusive license to produce a play. Lord Strange's Men will work to get the license for Shakespeare's tragedy *King Richard III* (or another early play of Shakespeare, as chosen by the GM), while the Lord Admiral's Men advocate for Marlowe's *Tragical History of Doctor Faustus* (or another Marlowe play).

The essential energy of the game lies in the contrast, visible in each meeting, between the somewhat lofty goals of humanist discourse, dramatic poetry, and pure, open entertainment of the theater on one hand and political maneuvers, pragmatic rhetoric, and the habitual secrecy of the court on the other. All players should be aware of the difficulty of crossing the ideal/real line, but all must manage it.

The major issues are artistic, intellectual, political, moral, and religious, as these would be understood by English people in the 1590s. What is most important in dramatic art: pleasing an audience, enriching an ancient tradition, or creating new and fresh experiences? Who should decide these questions: highly educated church-men and noblemen, or a rising class of newly literate people? Does the unlettered common man or woman have a voice we should heed? What is the place of soldierly valor or courtly gentility in an ever more urbanized and professionalized society? How far dare we take speech or spectacle that could disturb religious stability? In sum, what makes good drama, and what could make the theater itself a force for the good?

RULES AND PROCEDURES

1. Arguments and evidence should always be based on historically sound facts and opinions, consistent with the best scholarship on life and thought in Elizabethan England in the 1590s.
2. In the meetings of the commission, the actors speak only when permitted by the chair, respecting the following protocols, to be enforced by Tilney.

a. Each session begins and ends with a prayer from Whitgift, who must bring his Bible every day. All participants stand while Whitgift prays. (Every prayer must conclude with "And God save our glorious Queen" or some variation thereof.) Whitgift may, after the initial prayer, on subsequent days grant that privilege to another council member (and he may do so either to honor or to pressure that member). Players should look at the Books of Homilies and the Book of Common Prayer to see what Whitgift might say, and how to respond to or honor his words.

b. The actors should bow their heads in deference when the Privy Council enters the room; actors stand at that point. Dame Eleanor should curtsy.

c. Actors address the council as "My Lord," and Tilney is "Master Tilney." The council should be polite, but never deferential to the troupes.

d. Tilney begins, after Whitgift's prayer, with a formal announcement of the day's activities, having drawn up the agenda in consultation with Coke.

e. Coke presents at the beginning of each session a brief report on the Queen's interest in the progress of the contest, with any advice or warnings she may have given.

f. Tilney conducts each debate session: keeps time, announces topics, gives ground rules, allows for adjournments, and gives room for rebuttals. Tilney also reports to the troupes and Indeterminates on the council's debates (without revealing any secrets), and announces the day's winner and the rationale for the council's decision. He and Coke in consultation answer petitions from the players.

PETITIONS: These are opportunities for players and council members to make a special argument, ask for an unorthodox favor, plead for an accommodation, or file a grievance. They must be submitted in writing (electronic format is acceptable, with copies to the GM) at least twelve hours before the next game session, or the session in which the petition is to be ruled upon. The troupes can petition en masse ("Lord Strange's Men request . . ."), or any individual member may submit a petition, but be advised that Tilney's and Coke's time is limited. Tilney and Coke will jointly rule on each petition as soon as possible after its submission.

3. Scheming, circulating rumors, character assassination, and bribery are historically sound and potentially effective methods for achieving one's goals, though history shows they involve high risks to oneself and one's faction.

4. All players, actors, and councillors, may circulate written communications at any time, during or between sessions, anonymously or not, beyond the bare requirements of speeches and performances.

5. Bribes and other incentives should be based only on forms of exchange defined in the role sheets, or approved on historical grounds by the GM.

OBJECTIVES AND VICTORY CONDITIONS

Objectives are specified in the role sheets. Broadly speaking, a player wins if the company he or she supports is licensed by the final vote.

PRODUCTION VALUES

While each company should make use of simple, expressive costumes and props, the performances of scenes should rely most on the powerful presentation of words and actions, not on technical or expensive gimmicks. The GM must forbid electronic or other anachronistic stage effects, although electronic communication outside the game venue is certainly permitted.

BASIC OUTLINE OF THE GAME

Two acting companies will compete to persuade the Privy Council to grant an exclusive license to produce a play. With the support of their patrons on the Privy Council, Lord Strange's Men will work to get the license for a play of Shakespeare's, and the Lord Admiral's Men for a play of Marlowe's.

Introduction and Background: Ideas and Words in London, 1592

Before the commission convenes, each student will be responsible for presenting a memorable explanation of important ideas in one of several influential texts that circulated among learned men in London in 1592. These texts, which offer lessons in history, philosophy, religion, and poetics, will provide some of the authority for arguments made about the plays in the Privy Council. This exposition may be done in a twenty-first-century seminar discussion, or in character in 1592, as determined by the GM. Your role sheet indicates which text you will present.

The student's job in this first presentation is to make clear to the class any powerful terms or ideas this particular text may offer, to be used by any player in the game. Presenters will not be limited to using their assigned texts in their own arguments later, as they may well find more compelling authority in other texts presented and discussed by other students.

Planning and Organizing: Company Meetings and Rehearsals

Soon after this introductory discussion of the historical texts and contexts of the game, each acting company will meet to organize its presentations to the Privy Council's special commission on the revels, first in disputations and interrogatories, and second in performances of scenes from the competing plays. Each player will receive not only one or more parts in a play, but also a specific topic for argument in the council's disputations about the plays, which come before the performances.

Disputation in the Commission on the Revels

The six Privy Council members, having read the plays being considered, will interrogate the two companies of players. Each player will promote his company's cause in formal arguments for the relative merits and demerits of the two plays. **These arguments will be conducted as three separate topics, based on the authority of contemporary texts to the extent possible. The topics will be (1) the moral, ethical, and religious quality of the works; (2) their political or social virtues, and their likely effect on order and national ideals; and (3) the plays' poetical and aesthetic qualities, and especially the way their superior language and stagecraft produce theatrical pleasure.**

The members of the council will cross-examine the arguments of the actors. Actors from the opposing companies may question each other, with permission of the commissioners. A written version of your argument (three to five pages) must be circulated to all players the night before the disputations.

The Circulation of Strategic Imaginative Writing

The interest and stakes in the disputation sessions and performances can be greatly augmented by the circulation of writing from various individuals before and after each session. Imaginative documents of praise, slander, rumor, invective, and so on should intensify as the game goes on. While interrogations in the council must be rigorously decorous out of respect for Her Majesty's crown servants, the publications that are posted in public and that circulate in the streets privately from hand to hand may sometimes depart from that decorum and indulge in a wide variety of rhetorical strategies typical of the times, from high-minded moral discourse and sophisticated satire to innuendo and scandal-mongering couched in private letters or penny broadsides. At some point during the game every player will circulate one or more pieces of historically apt imaginative writing (totaling two to five pages). The GM should receive the original of any such writings, and can be enlisted to circulate it to the class anonymously as needed. See Assignments below.

Performance of Scenes for the Commission

Each troupe will perform selected scenes for the council. Each troupe should provide a set of suitable prologues, to be composed and spoken by a player who otherwise has few lines to perform. The prologue to each scene should provide the necessary narrative background, and should also exercise rhetorical flourish suited to the scene and the persuasive task at hand.

Troupes may be censured by Tilney and the commission for cutting or avoiding controversial scenes. The point of the hearings is to reveal the workings of these plays, not to misrepresent them.

The performances will be staged readings, but they should be interpretive, and theatrically exciting. Creativity and resourcefulness, within limits, will be rewarded. Troupes may and should bring costumes, props, music, or any particular talents they possess for the purpose of making a strong, favorable dramatic impression. Each actor should have memorized at least one important speech to deliver with special emphasis for dramatic effect.

The Final Vote, and After

The members of the commission will read their summary judgments, which take the form of reasoned arguments, in form like the ones actors have presented in disputations (three to five pages). Then a vote will be taken to license one play.

Alternatively, at the discretion of the GM, the entire assembly may vote, with the Privy Council's votes worth *five* votes apiece; everyone else's vote counts as one. The rationale for this alternative is to increase the stakes for troupes to maintain their unity of purpose and avoid defections, as well as to offer some reward for their labor, while acknowledging the power differential in the society.

One troupe may thus gain official supremacy for primarily literary but also cultural, religious, and political reasons. This will conclude the council-sponsored competition for "playspace," in effect awarding an exclusive theater contract with Philip Henslowe's Rose Theatre.

The losing company may in some measure recover their fortunes in the time between the vote and the debriefing meeting. Each company should designate one player who will present an appeal to Tilney at this point in the event of losing the vote. This is a good opportunity for members who want to make a more prominent contribution, through writing and networking, than they have done so far in this game.

A losing company can also find another playhouse in which to perform, producing a convincing appeal from the playhouse owner or manager (discovered through research) to Tilney for a special license.

As a consolation prize, Tilney may issue a temporary license for the losing company to perform the play they presented (or another, for fewer points) at court for the Christmas revels. One of the council members may engage the losing company likewise for private performances on his own.

If an individual actor's performance is sufficiently distinguished, he may be asked by Tilney to join the Queen's retinue or household, not an unhappy reward.

Tilney's announcement of the vote and the consolation awards will end the game.

ASSIGNMENTS

For Introductory Sessions:
Read and Present the Background Texts

Compose and deliver **a presentation on one or more of the background texts**, as assigned to you in your role sheet. The readings can give the class important clues about your character and position in the world of the game. Your presentation, only three to five minutes long, must emphasize each text's main ideas and the ways that it might inform arguments in the game. Your instructor may require a written version of this presentation (two to four pages), or may prefer to grade it as an oral presentation only.

For the Company Meetings and Rehearsals: Read the Plays to Choose Scenes and Evidence

Before the first company meeting, read the play you will support in the game. As you read, look for winning scenes, the ones that will be most appealing to your audience in the performances. The plays have exciting plots and characters, but the language may be a challenge. Do not hesitate to **get help from scene-by-scene summaries**, widely available online or in print. It is not cheating to **watch a performance of your play** before you read; that's how audiences in 1592 would have experienced the plays first. Several good video recordings are available. You may even want to organize a viewing party with other members of your company. Come to the company meeting ready to advocate for one or more scenes for your company's performance.

Between rehearsals and disputations, read the **play you will oppose**, using summaries and video to help you identify scenes and lines that are vulnerable to attack on artistic, political, ethical, or religious grounds.

For the Disputations and Interrogatories before the Privy Council: Make an Argument

Compose and deliver a closely reasoned argument (three to five pages) for the virtues and artistic superiority of one of the plays, or the vices and inferiority of the other, based on values current in 1592. This will require the use of memorable evidence from the texts of the plays and historical authority from the background texts. Consult your role sheet for advice on sharing the writing, research, and speaking duties with company members and allies, as appropriate to your role. Each acting company will use part of its initial organizing meeting to decide how to distribute topics among its members. Your argument will provide one major writing grade.

Between Sessions throughout the Game and at the Performances: Circulate Imaginative Writing

Compose one or more pieces of strategic imaginative writing (totaling two to five pages), for circulation (electronically or in hard copy) publicly, anonymously, or secretly. These writings may include sensational propaganda or posters, broadside ballads, sonnets, letters of petition, secret proposals for a plot or stratagem, or introductions and bridging narrations or additional speeches to be included in your performance. You should coordinate the timing of these writings with your allies so that a steady stream, two or three at a time, appears from your company throughout the play of the game. Anonymous writings should be sent to the GM to be distributed without your name attached; secret communications between players should be copied to the GM.

When you write your speeches and pamphlets and your secret missives to one another, try to write as much as you can in Elizabethan language and idiom. **Use the core readings as your guide.** Any outbursts of modern slang or language in the modern tongue will be penalized by Coke with a warning, then with the removal of the offending player if his language is not mended.

4

Roles and Factions

Privy Council/Commission for the Revels
William Cecil, Lord Burghley, secretary of state
Robert Devereux, Earl of Essex
Edmund Tilney, master of the Queen's revels (chair)
Robert Cecil, assistant secretary of state
John Whitgift, Archbishop of Canterbury
Master Edward Coke, solicitor general — *Represents Queen Elizabeth*
Indeterminate: Eleanor Bull, tavern owner, gatherer

Lord Admiral's Men (Marlowe's Acting Company)
Edward Alleyn, principal actor and celebrity
Thomas Downton, actor and Alleyn understudy
Anthony Munday, hack writer and comic actor
Thomas Dekker, actor, playwright, pamphleteer
Thomas Kyd, actor, playwright, Marlowe's roommate
1. Richard Jones, actor and printer
2. Thomas Gough, actor of minor roles and prompter for the troupe

Lord Strange's Men (Shakespeare's Acting Company)
Richard Burbage, principal actor
× Will Kemp, clown
Richard Cowley, actor, player of bit parts
Henry Condell, actor and archivist/editor
George Bryan, veteran actor, specialist in female roles
Thomas Pope, actor and aspiring writer
John Heminge, actor and prompter
Augustin Phillips, veteran actor and musician

THE WORK OF THE PRIVY COUNCILLORS

If it seems to the players that the Privy Councillors get a plum assignment because they don't have to act in scenes but merely sit in judgment, recall that they have to conduct daily interrogation, make speeches, take part in the debate, and conduct relentless intrigue for their own causes. Players on the council have by far the most research to do, as they need to have foreseen and *already* taken apart the lowly actors' arguments before they make them. **And the players on the council will also have to prepare themselves to perform a brief, noble entertainment at the Queen's command.**

The council is governed by a sense of propriety and decorum but capable of trickery and not immune to using its own prejudices to perceive and shape the world in a certain way. Their job is very heavily research based: by studying the biographies here, they have to figure out which prejudices each of their own characters is likely to have.

The Privy Councillors

As the leader of the English clergy, **John Whitgift, Archbishop of Canterbury**, is committed to religious stability according to the moderate compromises between ultra-Protestants and moderates, as worked out in the early days of Queen Elizabeth's reign. Churchmen, though conservative in many ways, may tend to support advancement by merit and learning (rather than by birth or military prowess). Clergymen also look on public entertainments with suspicion and hostility, as these may present moral dangers.

Robert Devereux, Earl of Essex, as a leading member of the titled nobility, can be assumed to respect social rank established by birth and warrior status, and to look with suspicion on men like **William Cecil, Lord Burghley, secretary of state**, the Queen's chief civil servant, and Burghley's son, **Sir Robert Cecil, assistant secretary of state**. Essex sees such men, who have risen by their learning and bureaucratic expertise, as educated "clerks," little better than the City men who have risen in trade and the practice of law. The old warrior nobility are apt to look on the common people as potential draftees for the army, otherwise as a dangerous rabble.

Crown servants **Master Edward Coke** and **Edmund Tilney** are, like the Cecils, individually ambitious, but also loyal to their patroness, the Queen. **Coke, the solicitor general**, is the Queen's

lawyer, and also the Speaker of the House of Commons. **Tilney, master of the Queen's revels**, is responsible for all royal entertainments, and has taken charge of supervising and censoring the rising business of public performances. These crown servants are above all committed to political and religious stability, though some may harbor secret sympathies for radical Protestant or even recusant Catholic views. Such self-made leaders understandably welcome the social mobility that allows men of talent in law or trade to rise in the social hierarchy. Although they may look on public entertainments with suspicion of civil disorder, they also enjoy a good time (and profits).

Factions in the Privy Council: Taking Sides

One of the most compelling subhistories of this period involves the hostility between Essex (Robert Devereux) and Robert Cecil, the Queen's assistant secretary of state. Cecil is the son of William Cecil, Lord Burghley, secretary of state, treasurer, and Queen's most trusted counselor. Cecil had his father's tutelage, fortune, and favor to rely on; Essex too was aristocratically born and protected, but he lived for some years under the wardship of Burghley himself after his father, Walter Devereux, requested that Burghley take care of the boy. The causes of the Essex-Cecil hostility are several, but pivot on the competition over place. Essex wishes for ever-more-important positions in the government, regards himself (and tries to behave) as a glorious soldier and chivalric hero, and certainly believes he is ripe for a position of greater administrative or political responsibility than he has yet received. But because the Queen has an interest in maintaining the factional balance of competing interests at court, his supremacy is hardly likely. He has yet to figure this out.

He makes a habit of petitioning Elizabeth for various favors, acting recklessly in response to those favors, and then taking offense when the Queen disciplines him. By way of contrast, Robert Cecil is a sly, subtle operator who could no more emulate Essex's flamboyance than he could run a

100-meter dash. Cecil is physically limited—he was born with a spinal deformity—and mentally formidable. But he is not a flatterer, and the Queen may not like him much. Essex and Cecil dislike and distrust each other, and will not typically agree on many issues. Nonetheless, they must work together, and they behave cordially on the surface. Their schemes to undermine each other are managed covertly.

It seems that the hostilities that broke out between Essex and Cecil later in the decade were merely latent and roiling in 1592; but assume they are present, though barely contained. All members of the Queen's ruling body have individual agendas, but they must also make choices together, at least in public. Their private deliberations must be polite, but when they have a point to make, they can insist on it, vigorously. Coke will adjudicate all disputes, and Tilney must not be intimidated here: he has as much right to speak as any other councillor, for the Queen has given him great powers over the theater. (In fact, Tilney is something of a resident expert, ready to teach the council about the actors and their plays.) For even though the Queen employs factionalism to maintain a balance of court influences, she cannot stand *overt* internecine strife—she sees it as a direct challenge to her rule. Coke has a range of punishments (in the form of written recommendations to the Queen) he will keep at hand and threaten to use to keep the council in line. A council member may even be excluded from the game if the transgressions are severe. Ejection will require Her Majesty's approval, as will any terms for reinstatement; Coke will report such events to the commission (in consultation with the GM).

The division between the young Essex and Cecil does not necessarily mean that Burghley will back his son's preferences. The son, rather, must follow the father, in despite of what Essex thinks. Burghley has residual loyalties to and affection for Essex, and he is always intensely concerned with what will be best for the Queen and the nation.

And here we have a genuine question. To oppose Essex—the Queen's favorite and the chief chivalric figure at court—is partly to oppose the Queen, even though Essex was always falling out of and then back into favor. Archbishop Whitgift tries to remain detached from these contests, but he has connections to both Essex and Burghley, the latter having helped advance Whitgift's career. Devereux's retreat from a strong pro-Puritan stance also pleases the archbishop. But can Essex be trusted? Is he not a will-o'-the-wisp, an unstable element at court? At the very least, he is a genuine power player whose affections and interests must be respected, and anyone who opposes him must tread carefully, for the game of influence is always perilous. Essex will exercise his power and place in as many ways as he possibly can. Coke, who may be well-disposed toward him, has recently become a bit nervous about Devereux's rash actions, but thinks he can be controlled. Except for Cecil, whose opposition is assured, the rest of the council (including Tilney) is undecided at the beginning of the game about the person and the prospects of Devereux.

Burghley and Whitgift have a history of tension between them, but they are not sworn enemies; mostly, they are uneasy rival advisers to the Queen. Both men jealously guard their turf. Indeed, Elizabeth installed Whitgift partly to counter the council's inattention (as she saw it) to questions of radical church reformers, those preachers and teachers who sought a Church of England entirely purged of Catholic influence or trappings. Whitgift, in particular, is a vicious tracker and persecutor of Puritans, and he managed to successfully thwart the elder Cecil's moderation on the question of Puritan arrest, torture, and execution. The Queen backed Whitgift, realizing (according to some) that the Puritans represented a profound threat to the realm, to her own monarchy, and to the Anglican compromise.

Coke, though not hostile to Whitgift, befriended many a Puritan over his long career. And furthermore, Coke seemed to take special delight in bringing down the "great," the uppity, the too powerful. He may, in other words, be hostile to the entire Privy Council, and may even try to thwart their desires as he understands them.

It may seem at first as if the Cecil faction wants to support Marlowe; certainly Burghley may have reason to do so. However, the Cecils may also wish to keep him out of the limelight. Would the Cecils be better off if Lord Strange's Men won? Would the Queen? Along these lines, Essex might wish to work for a Marlowe victory for reasons that lie below the surface. He would like to expose the dealings of his rival every bit as much as he would like to advance his own cause, for to damage his enemies (at least, younger Cecil) *is* his cause. Tilney, of course, stays and is kept out of these intrigues as much as possible.

The Privy Council must not only respond quickly to the actors' arguments, including rebuttals and counterrebuttals (which means, again, that they must be prepared to know the arguments), but will also in closed sessions have to decide, individually and collectively, on petitions from the troupes and the Indeterminates for all sorts of things: favor, money, extra time, patronage, or merely the right to be heard with an extra speech or an individual performance or two. Coke will help the council decide collective petitions; most individual petitions must be adjudicated individually.

Generally, the goal of a Privy Councillor was to defend the monarch and the nation. But he also sought to curry favor with the Queen, or to "master" her somehow; pleasing her was the best way to that end. So each member must try to decide which of the troupes would be the most effective mouthpiece for the Queen; or, alternatively, which would provide her the best entertainment. In any case, the Privy Council will not "win" as a group; they are driven by faction, and so will probably split their vote. The only way they could agree unanimously is by coincidence (each man having a different rationale for what turns out to be the same choice), or if one acting troupe is so inept as to be nearly tragically in the wrong profession. In

such a case, no councillor would embarrass himself by recommending that troupe.

Such a case should not arise.

At the same time, and while each councillor always serves at the pleasure of the Queen, each has his own power to consider, his own position. The playwright or company that would best serve in that capacity will doubtless win favor. It is not impossible that a troupe or playwright a councillor thought he would back at the beginning might turn out to be an embarrassment, and then he might well vote against his initial best guess.

THE ACTORS AND THEIR TROUPES

Unless otherwise noted in the role sheets, assume for the purposes of the game that each actor's alliance with and support of his acting troupe is sincere, at least at first. However, all actors seek better employment, so it is not necessarily the case that the players are fully loyal to their troupes. Indeed, actors, your final vote is entirely up to you, and the contest may encourage you to strike deals with opposing troupes or lords who may not support your troupe, as far as you can tell. But remember, your chances of (financial) success and security are better with your troupe than out on your own. Furthermore, life is dangerous for unemployed actors; they are subject to the national laws against rogues and vagabonds. So be careful, and be certain. Lords and nobles will use you at their pleasure in order to gain what many men desire; they are not, on balance, to be trusted. Whatever your alliances, you must put forth the strongest acting effort possible so that prospective patrons and future employers (and Coke, therefore the Queen) are impressed with you. It will avail you nothing to perform poorly, or in conscious sabotage of your troupe if, for some reason, you are not dedicated to that troupe, or if you have been won away by tangible rewards or promises of the same. And the Privy Council members are not stupid: they know that if you are treacherous enough to betray your troupe, you are just as likely to betray them.

Hardship could drive you to extreme measures. You may have links to the writing and publishing trades in London, and you may have to work in various capacities outside your own trade to make ends meet.

One highly effective strategy is to accuse your opponents (or their writer) of being what they are—*actors* and *playwrights*. This gambit resembles that of political campaigns in which one side accuses the other of being *politicians*. In other words, rely on the common pejorative and unpleasant connotations of the stage to accuse your opponent of what you both are. For many antitheatrical sources and useful quotations to deploy or imitate, see E. K. Chambers, *The Elizabethan Stage*, and Jonas Barish, *The Antitheatrical Prejudice*; and, for a contemporary source, see Philip Stubbes, *Anatomy of Abuses* (1583).[1] Unsurprisingly, the Puritans had the greatest number and range of objections to the stage. Perhaps their main objection to Catholicism, in fact, was that it was too *theatrical*: too dependent on costumes, ceremony, and scripts (such as nonspontaneous prayers and dry, oft-repeated rituals). There are Puritan sympathizers on the Privy Council, but no declared Puritans, of course. The troupes will have the challenge of accusing one another in the language of Puritans without seeming to damn their own practice!

Before and during the interrogatories, actors must meet often with their companies in order to prepare their arguments and any rebuttals the council allows. Indeterminates should write appeals and requests to the council, their patrons, and Coke, asking to be heard on a particular subject, or to request a private audience with a council member. The troupes would also do well to remind the council discreetly of something that one of the writers was later to mention: the

players should be treated well, because "they are the abstract and brief chronicles of the time. After your death you were better have a bad epitaph than their ill report while you live" (*Hamlet*, act 2, scene 2).

Performances

In the illustrative skits and the final performances, the troupes must attend to one crucial element of the game: you must try to emulate early modern acting styles. Such styles seemed (at the time of our game) to be falling between loud bluster and bombast for the heroic roles and introspective, psychologized acting as practiced in the last several decades in American and British theater and cinema. In terms of stage presentation, Marlowe's grand, outsized heroes and villains would probably require a "hammier" presentation; in Marlowe, too, the distance between the *appearance* of hero and villain (or protagonist and antagonist) would generally be easier to see than in Shakespeare, but that may merely be modern prejudice talking.

What about the final performance? Though it appeared a decade after our game, Hamlet's advice to the players in his temporary employ may be relevant here:

> Speak the speech, I pray you, as I pronounced it to you, trippingly on the tongue: but if you mouth it, as many of your players do, I had as lief the town crier spoke my lines. Nor do not saw the air too much with your hand, thus, but use all gently: for in the very torrent, tempest, and, as I may say, whirlwind of passion, you must acquire and beget a temperance that may give it smoothness. O, it offends me to the soul, to hear a robustious periwig-pated [= boisterous, wigheaded] fellow tear a passion to tatters, to very rags, to split the ears of the groundlings, who, for the most part, are capable of nothing but inexplicable dumb shows [= mime shows] and noise. . . . Be not too tame neither; but let your own discretion be your tutor: suit the action to the

1. E. K. Chambers, ed., *The Elizabethan Stage*, vols. 1 and 4 (Oxford: Clarendon, 1951); Jonas Barish, *The Antitheatrical Prejudice* (Berkeley: University of California Press, 1981), 1.

word, the word to the action; with this special observance, that you o'erstep not the modesty of nature: for anything so overdone is from the purpose of playing, whose end, both at the first and now, was and is, to hold, as 'twere, the mirror up to nature; to show virtue her own feature, scorn her own image, and the very age and body of the time his [= its] form and pressure. (*Hamlet*, act 3, scene 2)

Hamlet goes on to reject the crowd-pleasing antics of clowns, but it may be guessed that he's simply not in the mood for fooling. Still, his advice can be helpful. Acting styles in the theater in this period seem to be undergoing a transition from the loud, declamatory style of bold speech and broad, exaggerated movements and gesticulations to a quieter, or at least more "naturalistic," style closer to "method" acting, which attempts to approximate realism or real-world emotions and reactions. Hamlet certainly does not believe that his players ought to try to suffer in a "real-life" fashion what their characters suffer—only, rather, that they play a convincing version of human beings on the stage, and not people who have memorized artificial lines that they are speaking artificially. It may be the case that Hamlet is rejecting the acting style made popular by the very dramatic, extremely impressive stage presence of none other than Ned Alleyn. But to take Hamlet's advice is (depending on the play) to reject his advice: suit the word to the action, and if the action is exaggerated enough, so must the word be. In any case, Alleyn's style of bold, heroic acting might, along with the parts written for it, have been going out of style just at the moment of this game. But if the figures of Tamburlaine and Doctor Faustus were both written for him, then he was clearly capable of a range of moods, of dramatic nuance—and of abiding popularity.

In general, be creative with your theatrical choices. Use all your resources within period limits: if you have in your troupe anyone who can play music, sing beautifully, write ballads, sew or piece together costumes; actors who can also do impressions; any jugglers or acrobats or dancers, employ their talents to the full!—don't worry if the display of skills makes sense in context. Find a forum or occasion to exercise all your talents. Try to get members of the audience to participate in your play; you could even ask the council to read some lines, with the proper gestures toward their dignity. Remember that clowns and fools were immensely popular on stage—a very famous one, Richard Tarleton, had recently died (1588), and he was one of Queen Elizabeth's favorites. Renaissance plays were multimedia events, or at least multigenre events: tragedies often ended with a dance, and almost all plays found a way to sneak in a few songs. Furthermore, plays were similar to modern film and theater performances in this sense: the star system operated, and one or more famous actors could successfully "open" a play.

You might consider having the fool perform a comic introduction to your tragedy—such mixing of genre did not bother the Elizabethans—or even having him play a tragic part. For instance, in a performance of *Titus Andronicus* or *The Jew of Malta*, either Shakespeare's Aaron or certainly Marlowe's Ithamore would be convincing (or convincingly menacing) as a villainous clown.

As best you can, memorize the scene or scenes that you plan to perform. The performance ought to be more than a mere recitation; it should be a "reading," an interpretive account, that shows your playwright to be unquestionably the best and most entertaining, profitable, and exciting in London. The more creative and arresting your performance, the better chance it will be preferred by the council. Godspeed, and the devil take the hindmost.

5

Core Texts and Documents

The Plays: The core texts of the game are two plays, one by Marlowe and one early play by Shakespeare, selected by the GM. These will provide you with the primary material for your arguments and performances. Which is the better play on stage, and which the better expression of the virtues of England's language, kingdom, and religion? As explained in chapter 3 in Assignments, you may rely on summaries and video performances to help with your reading and selection of winning scenes, but by the beginning of the disputations you must know both plays well enough to draw directly from the text for your arguments and performances.

Background Texts and Documents: Your arguments must be based on values or viewpoints current in England in 1592, though these were often debated at the time. Each player should also rely on one or more of the following texts, important documents of early modern culture that Privy Councillors would plausibly have known in 1592.

For the specific purposes of the game, ask how each author's ideas could be used to justify (or condemn) the moral, political, and literary qualities of each of the plays we consider. Be advised that you will not be able to deploy all of the information you acquire in the game debates themselves. Your supplementary written arguments will afford you many opportunities to deepen your position and make it more convincing.

The headnotes to the readings provide important clues to broad issues of political and religious conflict and specific points of artistic, historical, and cultural relevance. These clues will help you locate passages in the texts that are apt to provide quotable precepts for your arguments in the disputations. But note too how these readings conflict with each other, and sometimes even with themselves.

DOCUMENTS OF RENAISSANCE LEARNING AND LITERATURE

How can we shape our own destinies by acquiring knowledge?

How should learning grace the language of our stage?

1. Pico della Mirandola, "On the Dignity of Man" (1486)

In his short life, the Italian philosopher Giovanni Pico della Mirandola (1463–94) caused a stir in the brilliant world of Medici Florence—and far beyond. His works in theology and philosophy are wide ranging and daring in their use of classical and Catholic texts, sometimes challenging medieval orthodoxies. His most famous work, the essay "On the Dignity of Man," is sometimes called "The Manifesto of the Renaissance," and is a foundation of the early modern movement that historians later called humanism.[1] Pico not only places man next to the angels in a "great chain of being," he also makes the revolutionary claim that God created man to determine his own nature. This claim both reflected and stirred contemporary ideas about how a human being could rise above (or fall below) the social expectations of birthright, particularly through the practice of literature and philosophy.♤

Most esteemed Fathers, I have read in the ancient writings of the Arabians that Abdala the Saracen on being asked what, on this stage, so to say, of the world, seemed to him most evocative of wonder, replied that there was nothing to be seen more marvelous than man. And that celebrated exclama-

---

1. **Humanism:** The *Oxford English Dictionary* defines this term, first used around 1850, as "a European intellectual movement or climate of thought from the 14th to the 16th cent., which was characterized in scholarship by attentiveness to classical Latin (and later Greek), in neo-Latin and vernacular literature by the creative imitation of ancient texts, in education and public life by the promotion of some or all of the wide range of cultural ideals which these texts were supposed to transmit, and in the fine and applied arts by creative response to Roman and Greek artefacts or principles." In the world of this game, humanist ideas have already transformed the education and rhetorical practices of leaders of church and state. Humanist ambitions appear most strongly here in characters like the Cecils or Coke, for whom learning and public administration are more important than chivalric nobility or theological debate.

---

tion of Hermes Trismegistus, "What a great miracle is man, Asclepius," confirms this opinion.

And still, as I reflected upon the basis assigned for these estimations, I was not fully persuaded by the diverse reasons advanced for the pre-eminence of human nature; that man is the intermediary between creatures, that he is the familiar of the gods above him as he is the lord of the beings beneath him; that, by the acuteness of his senses, the inquiry of his reason and the light of his intelligence, he is the interpreter of nature, set midway between the timeless unchanging and the flux of time; the living union (as the Persians say), the very marriage hymn of the world, and, by David's testimony but little lower than the angels. These reasons are all, without question, of great weight. Nevertheless, they do not touch the principal reasons, those, that is to say, which justify man's unique right for such unbounded admiration. Why, I asked, should we not admire the angels themselves and the beatific choirs more? At long last, however, I feel that I have come to some understanding of why man is the most fortunate of living things and, consequently, deserving of all admiration; of what may be the condition in the hierarchy of beings assigned to him, which draws upon him the envy, not of the brutes alone, but of the astral beings and of the very intelligences which dwell beyond the confines of the world. A thing surpassing belief and smiting the soul with wonder. Still, how could it be otherwise? For it is on this ground that man is, with complete justice, considered and called a great miracle and a being worthy of all admiration.

Hear then, oh Fathers, precisely what this condition of man is; and in the name of your humanity, grant me your benign audition as I pursue this theme.

God the Father, the Mightiest Architect, had already raised, according to the precepts of His hidden wisdom, this world we see, the cosmic dwelling of divinity, a temple most august. He had already adorned the supercelestial region with Intelligences, infused the heavenly globes with the life of immortal souls and set the fermenting dung-heap of the inferior world teeming with every form of animal life. But when this work was done, the Divine Artificer still longed for some creature which might comprehend the meaning of so vast an achievement, which might be moved with love at its beauty and smitten with awe at its grandeur. When, consequently, all else had been completed (as both Moses and Timaeus testify), in the very last place, He bethought Himself of bringing forth man. Truth was, however, that there remained no archetype according to which He might fashion a new offspring, nor in His treasure-houses the wherewithal to endow a new son with a fitting inheritance, nor any place, among the seats of the universe, where this new creature might dispose himself to contemplate the world. All space was already filled; all things had been distributed in the highest, the middle and the lowest orders. Still, it was not in the nature of the power of the Father to fail in this last creative élan; nor was it in the nature of that supreme Wisdom to hesitate through lack of counsel in so crucial a matter; nor, finally, in the nature of His beneficent love to compel the creature destined to praise the divine generosity in all other things to find it wanting in himself.

At last, the Supreme Maker decreed that this creature, to whom He could give nothing wholly his own, should have a share in the particular endowment of every other creature. Taking man, therefore, this creature of indeterminate image, He set him in the middle of the world and thus spoke to him:

"We have given you, O Adam, no visage proper to yourself, nor endowment properly your own, in order that whatever place, whatever form, whatever gifts you may, with premeditation, select, these same you may have and possess through your own judgement and decision. The nature of all other creatures is defined and restricted within laws which We have laid down; you, by contrast, impeded by no such restrictions, may, by your own free will, to whose custody We have assigned you, trace for yourself the lineaments of your own nature. I have placed you at the very center of the world, so that from that vantage point you may with greater ease glance round about you on all that the world contains. We have made you a creature neither of heaven nor of earth, neither mortal nor immortal, in order that you may, as the free and proud shaper of your own being, fashion yourself in the form you may prefer. It will be in your power to descend to the lower, brutish forms of life; you will be able, through your own decision, to rise again to the superior orders whose life is divine."

Oh unsurpassed generosity of God the Father, Oh wondrous and unsurpassable felicity of man, to whom it is granted to have what he chooses, to be what he wills to be! The brutes, from the moment of their birth, bring with them, as Lucilius says, "from their mother's womb" all that they will ever possess. The highest spiritual beings were, from the very moment of creation, or soon thereafter, fixed in the mode of being which would be theirs through measureless eternities. But upon man, at the moment of his creation, God bestowed seeds pregnant with all possibilities, the germs of every form of life. Whichever of these a man shall cultivate, the same will mature and bear fruit in him. If vegetative, he will become a plant; if sensual, he will become brutish; if rational, he will reveal himself a heavenly being; if intellectual, he will be an angel and the son of God. And if, dissatisfied with the lot of all creatures, he should recollect himself into the center of his own unity, he will there become one spirit with God, in the solitary darkness of the Father, Who is set above all things, himself transcend all creatures.

Who then will not look with awe upon this our chameleon, or who, at least, will look with greater admiration on any other being? This creature, man, whom Asclepius the Athenian, by reason of this very mutability, this nature capable of transforming itself, quite rightly said was symbolized in the mysteries by the figure of Proteus. This is the source of those metamorphoses, or transformations, so celebrated among the Hebrews and among the Pythagoreans; for even the esoteric theology of the Hebrews at times transforms the holy Enoch into that angel of divinity which is sometimes called malakh-ha-shekhinah and at other times transforms other personages into divinities of other names; while the Pythagoreans transform men guilty of crimes into brutes or even, if we are to believe Empedocles, into plants; and Mohammed, imitating them, was known frequently to say that the man who deserts the divine law becomes a brute. And he was right; for it is not the bark that makes the tree, but its insensitive and unresponsive nature; nor the hide which makes the beast of burden, but its brute and sensual soul; nor the orbicular form which makes the heavens, but their harmonious order. Finally, it is not freedom from a body, but its spiritual intelligence, which makes the angel. If you see a man dedicated to his stomach, crawling on the ground, you see a plant and not a man; or if you see a man bedazzled by the empty forms of the imagination, as by the wiles of Calypso, and through their alluring solicitations made a slave to his own senses, you see a brute and not a man. If, however, you see a philosopher, judging and distinguishing all things according to the rule of reason, him shall you hold in veneration, for he is a creature of heaven and not of earth; if, finally, a pure contemplator, unmindful of the body, wholly withdrawn into the inner chambers of the mind, here indeed is neither a creature of earth nor a heavenly creature, but some higher divinity, clothed in human flesh.

Who then will not look with wonder upon man, upon man who, not without reason in the sacred Mosaic and Christian writings, is designated sometimes by the term "all flesh" and sometimes by the term "every creature," because he molds, fashions and transforms himself into the likeness of all flesh and assumes the characteristic power of every form of life? This is why Evantes the Persian in his exposition of the Chaldean theology, writes that man has no inborn and proper semblance, but many which are extraneous and adventitious: whence the Chaldean saying: "Enosh hu shinnujim

vekammah tebhaoth haj"—"man is a living creature of varied, multiform and ever-changing nature."

But what is the purpose of all this? That we may understand—since we have been born into this condition of being what we choose to be—that we ought to be sure above all else that it may never be said against us that, born to a high position, we failed to appreciate it, but fell instead to the estate of brutes and uncomprehending beasts of burden; and that the saying of Aspah the Prophet, "You are all Gods and sons of the Most High," might rather be true; and finally that we may not, through abuse of the generosity of a most indulgent Father, pervert the free option which he has given us from a saving to a damning gift. Let a certain saving ambition invade our souls so that, impatient of mediocrity, we pant after the highest things and (since, if we will, we can) bend all our efforts to their attainment. Let us disdain things of earth, hold as little worth even the astral orders and, putting behind us all the things of this world, hasten to that court beyond the world, closest to the most exalted Godhead. There, as the sacred mysteries tell us, the Seraphim, Cherubim and Thrones occupy the first places; but, unable to yield to them, and impatient of any second place, let us emulate their dignity and glory. And, if we will it, we shall be inferior to them in nothing.

Translated from Latin by Richard Hooker (1994), http://public.wsu.edu/~brians/world_civ/worldcivreader /world_civ_reader_1/pico.html.

2. Ecclesiastes on the Vanity of Learning, from the Bishop's Bible (1568)

Leaders of the Elizabethan Church of England commissioned a scholarly translation of the Bible into English, in keeping with the Protestant principle that the scripture should be readily available to all believers. Ironically perhaps, this great work of scholarship includes this powerful indictment of vainly seeking after knowledge. ✆

I my selfe the preacher was kyng of Israel at Hierusalem [1:13] And dyd applie my mynde to seke out & searche for knowledge of all thynges that are done vnder heauen: Such trauayle and labour hath God geuen vnto the children of men, to exercise them selues therin ¹⁴ Thus have I considered all these thynges that come to passe vnder the sunne: and lo, they are all but vanitie and vexation of mynde ¹⁵ The croked can not be made straight, nor the imperfection of thynges can be numbred ¹⁶ I communed with myne owne heart, saying: lo I am come to great estate, and have gotten more wisdome then all they that have ben before me in Hierusalem ¹⁷ Yea, my heart had great experience of wisdome & knowledge: for thervnto I applied my mynde, that I myght knowe what were wisdome and vnderstandyng, what were errour and foolishnesse: and I perceaued that this was also but a vexation of mynde ¹⁸ For where much wisdome is, there is also great trauayle and disquietnesse: and the more knowledge a man hath, the more is his care ²:¹ Then sayde I thus in my heart: Nowe go to, I will take myne ease, and have good dayes: But lo, that is vanitie also ² Insomuch that I saide vnto the man geuen to laughter, thou art mad: and to mirth, what doest thou ³ So I thought in my heart to geue my fleshe vnto wine, and agayne to apply my mynde vnto wisdome, and to comprehende foolishnesse: vntyll the tyme that among all the thynges which are vnder the sunne, I myght see what were best for men to do so long as they liue vnder heauen ⁴ I made gorgious faire workes: I builded my houses, and planted vineyardes ⁵ I made me orchardes and gardens of pleasure, and planted trees in them of all maner of fruites ⁶ I made pooles of water, to water the greene and fruitfull trees withall ⁷ I bought seruauntes and maydens, and had a great housholde: As for cattel and sheepe, I had more substaunce of them then all they that were before me in Hierusalem ⁸ I gathered together siluer and golde, and the chiefe treasures of kynges and landes: I have prouided me men singers and women singers, and the delites of the sonnes of men, as a woman taken captiue, and women taken captiues ⁹ And I was greater and in more worship then all my predecessours in Hierusalem: For wisdome remayned with me ¹⁰ And loke whatsoeuer myne eyes desired, I let them have it: and wherin soeuer my heart delited or had any pleasure, I withhelde it not from it: Thus my heart reioyced in all that I did, and this was my portion of all my trauayle ¹¹ But when I considered all the workes that my handes had wrought, and all the labour that I had taken therin: lo all was but vanitie and vexation of mynde, and nothing of any value vnder the sunne ¹² Then turned I me to consider wisdome, errour, and foolishnesse (for what is he among men that myght be compared to me the kyng in such workes? ¹³ And I sawe that wisdome excelleth foolishnesse, as farre as light doth darknesse ¹⁴ For a wise man hath his eyes in his head, but the foole goeth in darknesse: I perceaued also that they both had one ende ¹⁵ Then thought I in my mynde, yf it happen vnto the foole as it doth vnto me, what needeth me then to labour any more for wisdome? So I confessed within my heart that this also was but vanitie ¹⁶ For the wise are euer as litle in remembraunce as the foolishe: for the dayes shall come when all shalbe forgotten: yea the wise man dyeth as well as the foole ¹⁷ Thus began I to be weery of my life, insomuch that I coulde away with nothyng that is done vnder the sunne: for all was but vanitie and vexation of mynde ¹⁸ Yea I was weery of my labour which I had taken vnder the sunne, because I shoulde be fayne to leaue them vnto another man that commeth after me ¹⁹ And who knoweth whether he shalbe a wise man or a foole? And yet shall he be lorde of all my laboures which I with such wisdome have taken vnder the sunne: This is also a vayne thyng ²⁰ So I turned me to refrayne my mynde from all such trauayle as I toke vnder the sunne ²¹ Forsomuch as a man shoulde weery hym selfe with wisdome, with vnderstandyng and oportunitie, and yet be fayne to leaue his labours vnto another that neuer sweat for them: This is also a vayne thyng, and great miserie ²² For what getteth a man of all the labour and trauayle of his mynde that he taketh vnder the sunne ²³ But heauinesse, sorowe, and disquietnesse all the dayes of his life? Insomuch that his heart can not rest in the nyght: This is also a vayne thing.

3. Erasmus and the New Learning

Desiderius Erasmus (1469?–1536), theologian and man of letters, had a strong influence on English school reform early in the Tudor century. Erasmus advocated schooling that combined the best classical authors with the highest Christian ideals, both applied not to abstruse reasoning but to practical problems of daily life and civic affairs. Erasmus dedicated one of his many writings on education, The Education of a Christian Prince, to the young Henry VIII, who had himself been schooled in such a curriculum. Indeed, all of Henry's children, including Queen Elizabeth, were educated on the principles of this so-called New Learning.

Erasmus tempers a conventional view of the sinful nature of man with an optimistic argument for the possibility of improvement by learning. He characterizes hereditary power and the courtly life in acerbic terms, but he holds out a rather sweet-natured hope that Aesop and Homer can teach the boy to be a virtuous prince. Note the humbling emphasis on the limitations of even the most powerful ruler.

Significantly, Erasmus describes learning as practice in the playing of roles and teaching as the telling of stories. ⌀

Since for the most part the nature of man inclines towards evil, and furthermore no nature is so blessed at birth that it cannot be corrupted by perverse training, how can you expect anything but evil from a prince who, whatever his nature at birth (and a good lineage does not guarantee a mind as it does a kingdom), is subjected from the very cradle to the most stupid ideas and spends his boyhood among silly women and his youth among whores, degenerate comrades, the most shameless flatterers, buffoons, street-players, drinkers, gamblers, and pleasure-mongers as foolish as they are worthless? In this company he hears nothing, learns nothing, and takes in nothing except

pleasure, amusement, pride, arrogance, greed, irascibility, and bullying, and from this schooling he is soon installed at the helm of his kingdom.

Since in all skills the highest are the most difficult, none is finer or more difficult than to rule well; why is it then that for this one skill alone we do not see the need for training but think a birthright is enough?

If as boys they did nothing but play at tyrants, what (I ask you) are they to work at as adults except tyranny? . . .

The teacher should make a start on his duties at once so as to sow the seeds of right conduct while the prince's understanding is still sensitive, while his mind is furthest removed from all vices and plastic enough to take on any form from the hand that moulds it. Wisdom has its period of infancy, as does piety. The teacher's objective is always the same, but he must use different methods at different times. While his pupil is still a little child, he can introduce into entertaining stories, amusing fables, and clever parables the things he will teach directly when the boy is older.

When the little pupil has enjoyed hearing Aesop's fable of the lion being saved in his turn by the good offices of the mouse, or of the dove protected by the industry of the ant, and when he has had a good laugh, then the teacher should spell it out: the fable applies to the prince, telling him never to look down on anybody but to try assiduously to win over by kindness the heart of even the humblest of the common people, for no one is so weak but that he may at some time be a friend who can help you or an enemy who can harm you, however powerful you may be yourself.

When he has had his fun out of the eagle, queen of the birds, who was almost totally destroyed by that very lowliest of insects the beetle, the teacher should again point out the meaning: not even the most powerful prince can afford to provoke or disregard even the humblest enemy. Often those who can do no harm physically can do so by guile.

When he has learned with pleasure the story of Phaethon, the teacher should show that he represents a prince who seized the reins of government in the headstrong enthusiasm of youth but with no supporting wisdom and brought ruin upon himself and the entire world.

When he has recounted the story of Cyclops, whose eye was put out by Ulysses, the teacher should say in conclusion that the prince who has great physical, but not mental, strength is like Polyphemus.

Who has not been glad to hear about how the bees and ants govern themselves? When the prince's childish mind has digested these tasty morsels, then his tutor should bring out whatever feature is educationally relevant, such as that the king never flies far afield since his wings are too small in proportion to his body, and that he alone has no sting. From this the lesson is drawn that it is the part of a good prince always to confine his activities within the limits of his realm and that clemency should be the quality for which he is particularly praised. . . .

What must be implanted deeply and before all else in the mind of the prince is the best possible understanding of Christ; he should be constantly absorbing his teachings, gathered together in some convenient form drawn from the original sources themselves, from this the teaching is imbibed not only more purely but also more effectively. Let him become convinced of this, that what Christ teaches applies to no one more than to the prince.

A large section of the masses are swayed by false opinions, just like those people trussed up in Plato's cave, who regarded the empty shadows of things as the things themselves. But it is the role of the good prince not to be impressed by the things that the common people consider of great consequence, but to weigh all things, considering whether they are really good or bad. But nothing is truly bad unless it is bound up with depravity, and nothing really good unless associated with moral worth. . . .

But at this point some idiot courtier, who is both more stupid and more misguided than any woman ever was, will protest: "You are making a philosopher for us, not a prince." "I am indeed making a prince," I reply, "although you would prefer a loafer like yourself to a prince. Unless you are a philosopher you cannot be a prince, only a tyrant. There is nothing better than a good prince, but a tyrant is such a bizarre beast that there is nothing as destructive, nothing more hateful to all."

From The Education of a Christian Prince *(1517; translated by Neil M. Cheshire and Michael J. Heath [Toronto: University of Toronto Press, 1974]).*

4. Christopher Marlowe on Ambition and Knowledge

Christopher Marlowe, son of a Canterbury shoemaker, rose through grammar school success to a scholarship at Cambridge University. There he developed a grand poetic and dramatic style, compounded of classical learning, powerful English verse, and a bounding imagination. The following passages display some of that learning in Marlowe's famous blank verse, and express a burgeoning confidence (and some confusion) about human aspirations.

Tamburlaine, who turned his tribal band into a conquering army that swept the steppes of central Asia, has conquered the mighty king of Persia. His exultation links the human capacity for knowledge to ambition for earthly power. ℧

From Tamburlaine the Great, Part One, *Act 2, Scene 6*

The thirst of reign and sweetness of a crown,
That caused the eldest son of heavenly Ops[1]
To thrust his doting father from his chair,
And place himself in th' empyreal heaven,
Moved me to manage arms against thy state.
What better precedent than mighty Jove?
Nature, that framed us of four elements
Warring within our breasts for regiment,
Doth teach us all to have aspiring minds.
Our souls, whose faculties can comprehend
The wondrous architecture of the world
And measure every wand'ring planet's course,
Still climbing after knowledge infinite,

1. Ops: Rhea, mother of Jove/Zeus, wife of Saturn/ Kronos, whom Zeus unseats by craft

And always moving as the restless spheres,
Wills us to wear ourselves and never rest,
Until we reach the ripest fruit of all,
That perfect bliss and sole felicity,
The sweet fruition of an earthly crown.

From The Tragical History of
Doctor Faustus, *Act 1, Scene 1*

*Faustus, a famous scholar of the University of
Wittenberg, contemplates the power and glory of
various kinds of learning: logic, medicine, law,
divinity. He rejects all these in favor of magic, which
he believes promises him most dominion.* ℧

FAUSTUS. Settle thy studies, Faustus, and begin
To sound the depth of that thou wilt profess:
Having commenced, be a divine in show,
Yet level at the end of every art,
And live and die in Aristotle's works.
Sweet Analytics, 'tis thou hast ravished me:
Bene disserere est finis logices.[1]
Is, to dispute well, logic's chiefest end?
Affords this art no greater miracle?
Then read no more, thou hast attained the end;
A greater subject fitteth Faustus' wit.
Bid *on kai me on*[2] farewell; Galen come:
Be a physician, Faustus, heap up gold,
And be eternized for some wondrous cure.
Summum bonum medicinae sanitas:[3]
The end of physic is our body's health.
Why Faustus, hast thou not attained that end?
Is not thy common talk sound aphorisms?
Are not thy bills hung up as monuments,
Whereby whole cities have escaped the plague,
And thousand desperate maladies been eased?
Yet art thou still but Faustus, and a man.
Couldst thou make men to live eternally,
Or, being dead, raise them to life again,

Then this profession were to be esteemed.
Physic farewell! Where is Justinian?[1]
Si una eademque res legatur duobus,
Alter rem alter valorem rei, etc.[2]
A pretty case of paltry legacies:
Exhereditare filium non potest pater nisi . . . [3]
Such is the subject of the Institute,
And universal body of the law:
This study fits a mercenary drudge
Who aims at nothing but external trash!
Too servile and illiberal for me.
When all is done, divinity[4] is best:
Jerome's Bible, Faustus, view it well:
Stipendium peccati mors est: ha! *Stipendium,* etc.[5]
The reward of sin is death? That's hard.
'Si pecasse negamus, fallimur,
Et nulla est in nobis veritas'.[6]
If we say that we have no sin,
We deceive ourselves, and there's no truth in us.
Why then belike we must sin,
And so consequently die.
Ay, we must die an everlasting death.
What doctrine call you this? *Che sera, sera:*[7]
What will be, shall be! Divinity, adieu!
These metaphysics of magicians,
And necromantic books are heavenly!
Lines, circles, schemes, letters and characters!
Ay, these are those that Faustus most desires.
O what a world of profit and delight,
Of power, of honour, of omnipotence
Is promised to the studious artisan!
All things that move between the quiet poles
Shall be at my command: emperors and kings
Are but obeyed in their several provinces,

---

1. "To argue well is the goal of logic."
2. "being and not being"
3. "The greatest good of medicine is health"

---

1. *Justinian:* Roman lawgiver
2. "If one thing is inherited by two people one shall have the thing, the other its value"
3. "A father may not disinherit a son unless . . ."
4. theology
5. translation immediately follows
6. translation immediately follows
7. translation immediately follows

Nor can they raise the wind, or rend the clouds;
But his dominion that exceeds in this
Stretcheth as far as doth the mind of man:
A sound magician is a mighty god.
Here Faustus, try thy brains to gain a deity.

5. Baldassare Castiglione, *The Book of the Courtier* (1528)

Baldassare Castiglione's witty and graceful "courtesy book" taught Renaissance ideals of manners to courtiers and would-be courtiers across Europe. It was more or less required reading for the aspiring courtier. Hoby's English translation was praised by the court tutor Roger Ascham, and the gallant poet-soldier Sir Philip Sidney carried a copy in his pocket. Here Castiglione urges that literary learning makes the aristocrat wise, but he also recommends plays and witty talk to give literary wisdom an aristocratic lightness, akin to sprezzatura, *the fashionable attitude of carefree confidence that he elsewhere recommends as the mark of the true gentleman.* ℘

On Learning (Book I, XLIII)

You know in great matters and aventurous in warres the true provocation is glory: and whoso for lucres sake or for any other consideration taketh it in hand (beside that he never doeth anye thynge worthy prayse) deserveth not the name of gentleman, but is a most vile marchaunt. And every man maye conceive it to be the true glorye, that is stored up in the holy treasure of letters, excepte such unlucky creatures as have had no taste thereof. What mind is so fainte, so bashefull and of so base a courage, that in reading the actes and greatnesse of Cesar, Alexander, Scipio, Hannibal, and so many other, is not incensed with a most fervent longing to be like them: and doth not preferred the getting of that perpetuall fame, before this rotten life that lastesth twoo dayes? Which in despite of death maketh him lyve a great deal more famous then before. But he that savoureth not the sweetnesse of letters, cannot know how much is the greatness of glorye, which is a longe whyle preserved by them,

and onely measureth it with the age of one or two men, for farther he beareth not in minde. Therefore can he not esteem this shorte glorye so much as he would do that which (in a maner) is everlastinge, if by his ille happe he wer not barred from the knowleage of it. And not passing upon it so much, reason perswadeth and man may well beleave he wyll never hazard hym self to come by it, as he that knoweth it. . . . Therefore . . . I will have [our courtier] to bee more than indifferently well seene, at the leaste in those studies, which they call Humanitie, and to have not only the understandinge of the Latin tunge, but also of the Greeke, because of the many and sundrye thinges that with greate excellencye are written in it. Let him much exercise hym selfe in poets, and no less in Oratours and Historiagraphers, and also in writing both rime and prose, and especiallye in this our vulgar tunge. For beside the contentation that he shall receive thereby himselfe, he shall by this meanes never want pleasaunt intertainements with women which ordinarily love such matters.

On Laughter and Play(s) (Book II, XLV–XLVI)

He is a livinge creature that can laugh: because this laughing is perceived only in man, and (in maner) always is a token of a certain jocundnesse, and merrie moode that he feeleth inwardlie in his minde, which by nature is drawn to pleasantness and coveteth quitnes and refreshing, for whiche cause we see menne have invented many matters, as sportes, games and pastimes, and so many sundrie sortes of open showes. And because we beare good will to suche as are the occasion of this recreation of oures, the maner was emonge the kinges of olde time, among the Romanes, the Athenians and manie other, to gete the good will of the people withal, and to feede the eyes and myndes of the multitude, to make greate Theatres, and other publyque buildings, and there to showe new devises of pastimes, running of horses and Charettes, fightinges of men together, straunge beastes, Comedies, Tragedies, and daunses of Antique. Neither did the grave Philosophers shonn these sightes, for manie tymes both in thys maner and at backettes they refreshed their weeryesome myndes, in those high discourses and divine imaginacions of theirs. The which in lykewyse all sortes of men are wyllinge to do, for not onlye Ploughmen, Mariners, and all such as are inured with harde and boisterous exercises, with hande, but also holye religious men and prisoners that from hour to hour waite for death, goe about yet to seeke some remedy and medicine to refreshe themselves. Whatsoever therefore causeth laughter, the same maketh the minde jocunde and geveth pleasure, nor suffreth a man in that instant to minde the troublesome greeffes that ourle life is full of. Therefore (as you see) laughing is very acceptable to all men, and he is muche to be commended that can cause it in due time after a comlie sort. . . . The place therefore and (as it were) the hedspring that laughing matters arise of, consisteth in a certein deformitie or ill favouredness, because a man laugheth onlie at those matters that are disagreeing in themselves, and (to a mans seeminge) are in yll plight, where it is not so in deede.[1]

> Translated ca. 1555 by Sir Thomas Hoby (brother-in-law of William Cecil, Lord Burghley)

6. Civic Pageantry: A Boy of Saint Paul's Grammar School Addresses the Queen in Her Coronation Procession

Saint Paul's School, founded early in the Tudor century, was a bastion of the revival of classical learning in the center of the City of London. Sons of the City's men of business learned Latin, and so learned to take their place in civic life. Throughout the Tudor century schoolboy actors competed with adult companies (as the actors in the Folio Hamlet complain), and boys of Saint Paul's were often

---

1. ". . . a man laugheth onlie at those matters that are disagreeing in themselves, and (to a mans seeminge) are in yll plight, where it is not so in deede": We laugh at things that seem to be inconsistent or even wrong, but are in fact so.

preeminent among them. Raphael Holinshed's account of one of the pageants in Queen Elizabeth's elaborate coronation procession gives a vivid picture of the interplay of classical schooling and civic pageantry, both strong influences on English drama. The theme of the pageant, "Truth is the daughter of time," makes a flattering reference to the long and hard wait Elizabeth endured before coming to the throne. ℘

[The author describes a mountain scene depicted on a pageant stage in the street near Saint Paul's Church and School:]

In the middle betweene the said hils, was made artificiallie one hollow place or cave, with doore and locke inclosed, out of the which, a little before the queenes highnesse comming thither, issued one personage, whose name was Time, apparelled as an old man, with a scythe in his hand, having wings artificiallie made, leading a personage of lesser stature than himselfe, which was finelie and well apparrelled, all clad in white silke, and directlie ouer her head was set her name and title in Latine and English, *Temporis filia*, The daughter of Time. Which two so appointed, went forwards toward the south side of the pageant. And on her brest was written her proper name, which was *Veritas*, Truth, who held a booke in her hand, upon the which was written *Verbum veritatis*, The word of truth. And out of the south side of the pageant was cast a standing for a child, which should interpret the same pageant [and] when the queenes maiestie came, he spake unto her grace these sweet words:

This old man with the scythe,
old father Time they call,
And her his daughter Truth,
which holdeth yonder booke:
Whome he out of his rocke,
hath brought foorth to us all,
From whence this manie yeares
she durst not once out looke.
The ruthfull wight that sits
vnder the barren tree,

Resembleth to us the forme,
when common weales decay:
But when they be in state
triumphant, you may see
By him in fresh attire,
that sits under the bay.[1]
Now since that Time againe,
his daughter Truth hath brought,
We trust ô worthie queene,
thou wilt this truth imbrace,
And since thou understandst,
the good estate and naught,
We trust wealth thou wilt plant,
and barrenness displace.
But for to heale the sore,
and cure that is not seene,
Which thing the booke of truth,
doth teach in writing plaine:
Shee doth present to thee
the same, ô worthie queene,
For that, that words doo fly,
but written dooth remaine.

When the child had thus ended his speech, he reached his booke towards the queenes maiestie, which a little before Truth had let downe vnto him from the hill, which by Sir Iohn Parrat was receiued, and deliuered vnto the quéene. But shée as soone as she had received the booke, kissed it, and with both her hands held vp the same, and so laid it vpon her brest, with great thanks to the citie therefore: and so went forward towards Paules churchyard. The former matter which was rehearsed vnto the queenes maiestie, was written in two tables, on either side the pageant eight verses, and in the middest, these in Latine:

[Verses in Latin explaining the meaning of a scene of two trees, representing a ruined commonwealth and a prosperous commonwealth]

The sentences written in Latine and English upon both the trées, declaring the causes of both

estates, and first of a ruinous commonweale were these: Want of Gods feare, disobedience to rulers, blindnesse of guides, briberie in magistrats, rebellion in subiects, civill discord, flattering of princes, unmercifulnesse in rulers, unthankefulnesse in subjects. Causes of a flourishing commonweale are these: Feare of God, a wise prince, learned rulers, obedience to officers, obedient subiects, louers of the commonweale, vertue rewarded, vice chastened.

The matter of this pageant dependeth of them that went before. For as the first declared her grace to come out of the house of Unitie, the second that she is placed in the seat of gouernement staid with vertues, to the suppression of vice; and therefore in the third, the eight blessings of almightie God might well be applied unto her: so this fourth now is, to put her grace in remembrance of the state of the commonweale, which Time with Truth his daughter dooth reueale: which Truth also her grace hath received, and therefore cannot but be mercifull and carefull for the good governement thereof. From thence, the queenes maiestie passed toward Paules churchyard, and when she came ouer against Paules schoole, a child appointed by the schoolemaister thereof, pronounced a certeine oration in Latine, and certeine verses, which . . . the queenes maiestie most attentivelie hearkened vnto. And when the child had pronounced, he did kisse the oration which he had there faire written in paper, and delivered it unto the queenes maiestie, which most gentlie received the same.

From Holinshed's Chronicles *(1586)*

7. An English Poetry in the Classical Tradition: Puttenham's *Art of English Poesy* (1589)

The Renaissance emphasis on the glories of Greek and Latin literature leads to a tough question: Can English compete with classical languages for beauty and depth of expression? George Puttenham's handbook for poetic composition relies heavily on classical models and forms, but affirms that England is ready now to produce its own poetic art.

---

1. *bay:* laurel tree, symbol of honor

He points out that even though English lacks the "feete" of classical verse (measured by vowel sounds), it has other advantages for making poetic music. Puttenham offers not only classical forms and devices, but advice on avoiding poetic "vices" like the overuse of alliteration, to which English writers may be inclined.

Puttenham also includes some sharp discriminations about insufficient or "barbarous" poetic language that players might use as a critical model in disputations.

He begins his book by explaining that a poet is a maker of such power as to deserve comparison to "creating gods," at the very least "excellent imitators." Then he addresses the queen, herself well known to have composed poetry. ⌀

But you (Madame) my most Honored and Gracious: if I should seeme to offer you this my deuise for a discipline and not a delight, I might well be reputed, of all others the most arrogant and iniurious: your selfe being alreadie, of any that I know in our time, the most excellent Poet. Forsooth by your Princely purse fauours and countenance, making in maner what ye list, the poore man rich, the lewd well learned, the coward couragious, and vile both noble and valiant. Then for imitation no lesse, your person as a most cunning counterfaitor liuely representing Venus in countenance, in life Diana, Pallas for gouernement, and Iuno in all honour and regall magnificence.

That there may be an Art of our English Poesie, as well as there is of the Latine and Greeke.

Then as there was no art in the world till by experience found out: so if Poesie be now an Art, & of all antiquitie hath bene among the Greeks and Latines, & yet were none, untill by studious persons fashioned and reduced into a method of rules & precepts, then no doubt may there be the like with us. And if th'art of Poesie be but a skill appertaining to utterance, why may not the same be with us aswel as with them, our language being no less copious pithie and significatiue then theirs, our concepts the same, and our wits no less apt to

deuise and imitate then theirs were? If againe Art be but a certaine order of rules prescribed by reason, and gathered by experience, why should not Poesie be a vulgar [= popular] Art with us as well as with the Greeks and Latines, our language admitting no fewer rules and nice diversities then theirs? but peradventure more by a peculiar[ity], which our speech hath in many things differing from theirs: and yet in the generall points of that Art, allowed to go in common with them: so as if one point perchance which is their feete [= metrical quantities] whereupon their measures stand, and in deede is all the beautie of their Poesie, and which feete we haue not, nor as yet never went about to frame (the nature of our language and wordes not permitting it) we have in stead thereof twentie other curious points in that skill more then they ever had, by reason of our rime and tunable concords or simphonie, which they neuer observed. Poesie therefore may be an Art in our vulgar, and that verie methodicall and commendable.

Some vices in speaches and writing are always intollerable, some others now and then borne withall by licence of approued authors and custome.

The foulest vice in language is to speake barbarously: this terme grew by the great pride of the Greekes and Latines, when they were dominatours of the world reckoning no language so sweete and ciuill as their owne, and that all nations beside them selues were rude and vnciuill, which they called barbarous: So as when any straunge word not of the naturall Greeke or Latin was spoken, in the old time they called it barbarisme, or when any of their owne naturall wordes were sounded and pronounced with straunge and ill shapen accents, or written by wrong ortographie, as he that would say with vs in England, a dousand for a thousand, isterday, for yesterday, as commonly the Dutch and French people do, they said it was barbarously spoken. The Italian at this day by like arrogance calleth the Frenchman, Spaniard, Dutch, English, and all other breed behither their mountaines Appennines, Tramountani, as who would say Barbarous. This terme being then so vsed by the auncient Greekes, there haue bene since, notwith-standing who haue digged for the Etimologie somewhat deeper, and many of them haue said that it was spoken by the rude and barking lan-guage of the Affricans now called Barbarians, who had great trafficke with the Greekes and Romanes, but that can not be so, for that part of Affricke hath but of late receiued the name of Burbarie, and some others rather thinke that of this word Barba-rous, that countrey came to be called Barbaria and but few yeares in respect agone. Others among whom is Ihan Leon a Moore of Granada, will seeme to deriue Barbaria, from this word Bar, twise iterate thus Barbar, as much to say as flye, flye, which chaunced in a persecution of the Arabians by some seditious Mahometanes in the time of their Pontif. Habdul mumi, when they were had in the chase, & driuen out of Arabia Westward into the countreys of Mauritania, & during the pursuite cried one vpon another flye away, flye away, or passe passe, by which occasion they say, when the Arabians which were had in chase came to stay and settle them selues in that part of Affrica, they called it Barbar, as much to say, the region of their flight or pursuite. Thus much for the terme, though not greatly pertinent to the matter, yet not vnpleasant to know for them that delight in such niceties.

Your next intollerable vice is solecismus or incongruitie, as when we speake false English, that is by misusing the Grammaticall rules to be obserued in cases, genders, tenses and such like, euery poore scholler knowes the fault & cals it the breaking of Priscians head, for he was among the Latines a principall Grammarian.

Ye haue another intollerable ill maner of speach, which by the Greekes originall we may call fonde affectation, and is when we affect new words and phrases other then the good speakers and writers in any language, or the custome hath allowed, & is the common fault of young schollers not halfe well studied before they come from the Vniuersitie or schooles, and when they come to their friends, or happen to get some benefice or other promotion in their countreys, will seeme to coigne fine wordes out of the Latin, and to vse new fangled speaches, thereby to shew themselues among the ignorant the better learned.

Another of your intollerable vices is that which the Greekes call Soraismus, & we may call the [mingle mangle] as when we make our speach or writinges of sundry languages vsing some Italian word, or French, or Spanish, or Dutch, or Scottish, not for the nonce or for any purpose (which were in part excusable) but ignorantly and affectedly as one that said vsing this French word Roy, to make ryme with another verse, thus.

O mightie Lord or ioue, dame Venus onely ioy,
Whose Princely power exceedes ech other
    heauenly roy.

The verse is good but the terme peevishly affected. . . .

Another of your intollerable vices is ill disposition or placing of your words in a clause or sentence: as when you will place your adiectiue after your sub-stantiue, thus: Mayde faire, widow riche, priest holy, and such like, which though the Latines did admit, yet our English did not, as one that said ridiculously.

In my yeares lustie, many a deed doughtie did I.

All these remembred faults be intollerable and euer vndecent. . . .

Ye haue another manner of composing your metre nothing commendable, specially if it be too much vsed, and is when our maker takes too much delight to fill his verse with wordes beginning with a letter, as an English rimer that said:

The deadly droppes of darke disdaine,
Do daily drench my due desartes.

And as the Monke we spake of before, wrote a whole Poeme to the honor of Carolus Caluus, euery word in his verse beginning with C, thus:

Carmina clarisonae Caluis cantate camenae.

Many of our English makers vse it too much, yet we confesse it doth not ill but pretily becomes the meetre, if ye passe not two or three words in one verse, and vse it not very much, as he that said by way of Epithete.

The smoakie sights: the trickling teares.

And such like, for such composition makes the meetre runne away smoother, and passeth from the lippes with more facilitie by iteration of a letter then by alteration, which alteration of a letter requires an exchange of ministery and office in the lippes, teeth or palate, and so doth not the iteration. . . .

Ye haue another vicious speech which the Greekes call Acyron, we call it the vncouthe, and is when we vse an obscure and darke word, and vtterly repugnant to that we would expresse, if it be not by vertue of the figures metaphore, allegorie, abusion, or such other laudable figure before remembred, as he that said by way of Epithete.

A dongeon deepe, a dampe as darke as hell.

Where it is euident that a dampe being but a breath or vapour, and not to be discerned by the eye, ought not to haue this epithete (darke,) no more then another that praysing his mistresse for her bewtifull haire, said very improperly and with an vncouth terme.

Her haire surmounts Apollos pride,
In it such bewty raignes.

Whereas this word raigne is ill applied to the bewtie of a womans haire, and might better haue bene spoken of her whole person, in which bewtie, fauour, and good grace, may perhaps in some sort be said to raigne as our selues wrate, in a Partheniade praising her Maiesties countenance, thus:

A cheare where loue and Maiestie do raigne,
Both milde and sterne, &c.

Because this word Maiestie is a word expressing a certain Soueraigne dignitie, as well as a quallitie of countenance, and therefore may properly be said to raigne, & requires no meaner a word to set him sooth by. So it is not of the bewtie that remaines in a womans haire, or in her hand or any other member: therfore when ye see all these improper or harde Epithets vsed, ye may put them in the number of [vncouths] as one that said, the flouds of graces: I haue heard of the flouds of teares, and the flouds of eloquence, or of any thing that may resemble the nature of a water-course, and in that respect we say also, the streames of teares, and the streames of vtterance, but not the streames of graces, or of beautie.

Also the Poet or makers speech becomes vicious and vnpleasant by nothing more than by vsing too much surplusage: and this lieth not only in a word or two more than ordinary, but in whole clauses, and peraduenture large sentences impertinently spoken, or with more labour and curiositie than is requisite. The first surplusage the Greekes call Pleonasmus, I call him [too full speech] and is no great fault, as if one should say, I heard it with mine eares, and saw it with mine eyes, as if a man could heare with his heeles, or see with his nose. We our selues vsed this superfluous speech in a verse written of our mistresse, neuertheles, not much to be misliked, for euen a vice sometime being seasonably vsed, hath a pretie grace,

For euer may my true loue liue and neuer die
And that mine eyes may see her crownde a Queene.

As, if she liued euer she could euer die, or that one might see her crowned without his eyes.

How can drama glorify England and her Queen?

8. The Glories of the Public Theaters: Henslowe's Repertory in 1592
Possibly our best evidence of the richness and variety of the English drama in the age of Marlowe and

Shakespeare is the record kept by Philip Henslowe, the owner and manager of various theater companies and other entertainment businesses, perhaps including animal baiting and brothels. His diary records payments and receipts for plays performed from 1592 to 1609, coincidentally the years of Shakespeare's greatest production. In the first few months of 1592, documented here, Shakespeare is still a relative newcomer. ♉

[Note: "Rd at" = "Received" as box office receipts for the day's play. The amounts are expressed in shillings (*s*, from Latin "solidus"), pence (*d*, from Latin "denarius"), and occasionally pounds (*li*, from Latin "libra"). As "j" is often used for "i," the first entry records receipts of seventeen shillings three pence.]

Jn the name of god Amen 1591 [= 1592 New Style]
beginge the 19 of febreary
my lord strangers mene a ffoloweth
1591

Rd at fryer bacvne the 19 of febrary satterdaye	xvij s iij d
Rd at mvlomvrco the 20 of febreary	xxix s
Rd at orlando the 21 of febreary	xyj s vj d
Rd at spanes comodye donne oracoe the 23 of febreary	xiij s vj d
Rd at syr John mandevell the 24 of febreary	xij s vj d
Rd at harey of cornwell the 25 of febreary 1591	xxxij s
Rd at the Jewe of malltuse the 26 of febrearye 1591	ls [l = 50]
Rd at clorys & orgasto the 28 of febreary 1591	xviij s
Rd mvlamvlluco the 29 of febrearye 1591	xxxiiij s
Rd at poope Jone the i of marche 1591	xv s
Rd at matchavell the 2 of marche 1591	xiiij s 15 d
Ne[w play] Rd at harey the vj the 3 of marche 1591	iij li xvj s 8 d
Rd at bendo & Richardo the 4 of marche 1591	xvj s
Rd at iiij playes in one the 6 of marche 1591	xxxj s vj d
Rd at hary vj the 7 of marche 1591	iij li
Rd at the lookinglasse the 8 of marche 1591	vij s
Rd at senobia the 9 of marche 1591	xxij s vj d
Rd at the Jewe of malta the 10 of marche 1591	lvj s
Rd at hary the vj the n of marche 1591	xxxxvij s vj d
Rd at the comodey of doneoracio the 13 marche 1591	xxviiij s
Rd at Jeronymo the 14 of marche 1591	iij li xj s
Rd at harey the 16 of marche 1591	xxxj s vj d
Rd at mvlo mvllocco the 17 of marche 1591	xxviij s vj d
Rd at the Jewe of malta the 18 of marche 1591	xxxix s
Rd at Joronymo the 20 of marche 1591	xxxviij s
Rd at constantine the 21 of marche 1591	xij s 30
Rd at Q Jerusallem the 22 of marche 1591	xviij s
Rd at harey of cornwell the 23 of marche 1591	xiij s vj d
Rd at fryer bacon the 25 of marche 1591	xv s vj d
E[a]ster	
Rd at the lockinglass the 27 of marche 1591	lv s
Rd at harey the vj the 28 of marche 1591	iij li viij s
Rd at mvlomvlucko the 29 of marche 1591	iij li ij s
Rd at doneoracio the 30 of marche 1591	xxxix 8
Rd at Jeronymo the 31 of marche 1591	iij li
Rd at mandefell the i of aprell 1591	xxx s
Rd at matchevell the 3 of aprell 1591	xxij s
Rd at the Jewe of malta the 4 of aprell 1591	xxxxiij s
Rd at harey the vj the 5 of aprell 1591	xxxxj s
Rd at brandymer the 6 of aprell 1591	xxij s
Rd at Jeronymo the 7 of aprell 1591	xxvj s

[The following are the plays recorded above. Note the variety of comedy, melodrama, history, and so on.]

Friar Bacon and Friar Bungay by Robert Greene

Muly Mullocco [? = *The Battle of Alcazar* by George Peele]

Orlando Furioso by Robert Greene

Don Horatio, or The Comedy of Jeronimo by an unknown author

The Spanish Tragedy [possibly also called *Jeronimo*] by Thomas Kyd

Sir John Mandeville by Henry of Cornwall, lost/author unknown

Jew of Malta by Christopher Marlowe

Cloris and Ergasto, lost/author unknown

Machiavel, lost/unknown

Pope Joan by Daborne [?]

Henry VI, Part I, by William Shakespeare

Bindo and Richardo, lost/unknown

Four Playes in One [a lost play of the Seven Deadly Sins?]

A Looking-Glass for London and England, by Thomas Lodge and Robert Greene

Zenobia, lost/unknown

Constantine, lost/unknown [on legendary king, father of Uther Pendragon?]

Jerusalem, unidentified

Brandimer, lost/unknown

> *From Philip Henslowe's Diary, ed. W. W. Greg (London, 1904).*

9. The Public Theaters on the South Bank of the Thames: A Rough Neighborhood

London's theaters for the common people were built outside the legal boundaries of the city itself, in an area known as the "liberties" for their freedom from civic law. The neighborhood also housed prisons, brothels ("stews"), gambling houses, and the bear-baiting arena.

John Stow, in A Survey of London (1603; ed. E. L. Kingsford [1908]), describes the ward of Southwark as a mix of tenements, churches, jails, palaces, abbeys, brothels, and bear gardens. He includes archival documents that show repeated attempts to control the disorder associated with this rather wayward suburb. ✍

Having treated of Wardes in London, on the North side the Thames (in number 25.) I am now to crosse ouer the said Riuer into the Borough of Southwark, which is also a Warde of London, without the walles, on the South side thereof. . . .

An Abbey. A Priory, A Colledge & Hospitall. A Lazar house. Parish churches.

The antiquities most notable in this Borough are these: first, for ecclesiasticall, there was Bermondsey, an Abbey of Blacke Monkes, S. Mary Oueries, a Priorie of Canons Regular, saint Thomas a colledge or Hospitall for the poore, & the Loke a Lazar house in Kent street. Parish churches, there haue been 6. wherof 5. do remaine. . . .

There be also these 5. prisons or Gaoles [= jails].

The Clinke on the Banke. The Compter in the late parrish church of S. Margaret. The Marshalsey. The Kinges Bench. And the white Lyon, all in long Southwarke.

Houses most notable be these.

The Bishop of Winchesters house. The Bishop of Rochesters house.

The Duke of Suffolks house, or Southwarke place.

The Tabard an Hosterie or Inne.

The Abbot of Hyde his house. The Prior of Lewes his house.

The Abbot of saint Augustine his house.

The Bridge house.

The Abbot of Battaile his house. Battaile bridge.

The stewes on the Banke of Thames.

And the Beare gardens there.

The Beare gardens.

Now to returne to the West banke, there be two Beare gardens, the olde and new places, wherein be kept Beares, Buls and other beastes to be bayted. As also Mastiues in seuerall kenels, nourished to baite them. These Beares and other Beasts are there bayted in plottes of ground, scaffolded about for the Beholders to stand safe. . . .

The Stewe on the bank side.

Next on this banke was sometime the Bordello or stewes, a place so called, of certaine stew houses priuiledged there, for the repaire of incontinent men to the like women, of the which priuiledge I haue read thus.

In a Parliament holden at Westminster the 8. of Henry the second, it was ordayned by the commons and confirmed by the king and Lords, that diuers constitutions for euer should bee kept within that Lordship or franchise, according to the olde customes that had been there vsed time out of mind. Amongst the which these following were some, vz.

That no stewholder or his wife should let or staye [= prevent] any single Woman to goe and come freely at all times when they listed. No single woman to be kept against her will that would leaue her sinne.

Not to keepe open his dores vpon the holydayes. Not to keepe any single woman in his house on the holy dayes, but the Bayliffe to see them voyded out of the Lordship.

No stewholder to receiue any Woman of religion, or any mans wife.

No single woman to take money to lie with any man, but shee lie with him all night till the morrow.

No man to be drawn or inticed into any stew-house.

The Constables, Balife, and others euery weeke to search euery stewhouse.

No stewholder to keepe any woman that hath the perilous infirmitie of burning [= venereal disease], nor to sell bread, ale, flesh, fish, wood, coale, or any victuals, &c.

. . . These allowed stewhouses had signes on their frontes, towardes the Thames, not hanged out, but painted on the walles, as a Boares heade, the Crosse keyes, the Gunne, the Castle, the Crane, the Cardinals Hat, the Bel, the Swanne, &c. I haue heard ancient men of good credite report, that these single women were forbidden the rightes of the Church, so long as they continued that sin-nefull life, and were excluded from christian buriall, if they were not reconciled before their death. And therefore there was a plot of ground, called the single womans churchyeard, appoynted for them, far from the parish church.

Stewhouses put downe.

In the yeare of Christ, 1546. the 37. of Henry the eight, this row of stewes in Southwarke was put downe by the kings commandement, which was proclaymed by sounde of Trumpet, no more to be priuiledged, and vsed as a common Brothel, but the inhabitants of the same to keepe good and honest rule as in other places of this realme, &c.

The next is the Clinke, a Gayle or prison for the trespassers in those parts, Namely in olde time for such as should brabble, frey, or breake the Peace on the saide banke, or in the Brothell houses, they were by the inhabitantes there about apprehended; and committed to this Gayle, where they were straightly imprisoned.

10. A Noble Entertainment for the Queen (1591)

The Queen took notice of the plays produced for the public and even invited the players to perform for her court revels, but she also enjoyed a very different kind of entertainment, lavishly produced for the royal pleasure with rich costumes, music, dancing, and fantastic staging devices. Noblemen competed to please the Queen with such spectacles, like the four days of "entertainments" produced by the Earl of Hertford when Elizabeth visited his estate in 1591 during her annual "progress" of visits to great houses across the country. This was the only truly accept-able kind of theater in which the nobility could partake. Each day in various parts of Hertford's estate, the Queen would encounter players and musicians richly arrayed as knights, nymphs, sea gods, poets, or shepherds, singing and dancing and reciting verses to the monarch. On the fourth and last day she encountered the Fairy Queen, who addressed Elizabeth as "Phoebe" and "Cynthia," names for the virgin goddess of the moon. ☙

The Fourth Daies Entertainment.

On Thursday morning, her Majestie was no sooner readie, and at her Gallerie window looking into the Garden, but there began three Cornets to play certaine fantastike dances, at the measure whereof the Fayery Quen came into the garden, dauncing with her maides about her. Shee brought with her a garland, made in form of an imperiall crowne; within the sight of her Majestie shee fixed [it] upon a silvered staff, and sticking the staffe into the ground, spake as followeth:

The Speech of the Fairy Quene to her Majestie.
I that abide in places under-ground,
Aureola, the Quene of Fairy land,
That every night in rings of painted flowers
Turne round, and carrell out of Elisaes name:
Hearing, that Nereus and the Sylvane gods[1]
Have lately welcomed your Imperiall Grace,
Open'd the earth with this enchanting wand,
To do my duety to your Majestie,
And humbly to salute you with this chaplet,
Given me by Auberon, the Fairy King.
Bright shining Phoebe, that in humaine shape,
Hid'st Heaven's perfection, vouchsafe t'accept it:
And I Aureola, belov'd of heaven,
(For amorous starres fall nightly in my lap)
Will cause that Heavens enlarge thy goulden dayes,
And cut them short, that envy at they praise.

After this speech, the Fairy Quene and her maides daunced about the Garden, singing a Song of sixe parts, with the musicke of an exquisite consort; wherein was the lute, bandora, base-violl, citterne, treble-violl, and flute. And this was the Fairies Song:

Elisa is the fairest Quene,
That ever trod upon this greene.
Elisaes eyes are blessed starres,
Inducing peace, subduing warres.
Elisaes hand is christal bright,

Her wordes are balme, her lookes are light.
Elisaes brest is that faire hill,
Where Vertue dwels, and sacred skill,
O blessed be each day and houre,
Where sweet Elisa builds her bowre.

This spectacle and musicke so delighted her Majesty, that she commanded to heare it sung and to be danced three times over, and called for divers Lords and Ladies to behold it: and then dismist the Actors with Thankes, and with a gracious larges, which of her exceeding goodnesse shee bestowed upon them.

Within an howre after her Majesty departed, with her Nobles, from Elvetham. It was a most extreame rain, and yet it pleased hir Majesty to behold and hear the whole action. On the one side of her way, as shee past through the parke, there was placed, sitting on the Pond side, Nereus and all the sea-gods, and in their former attire: on her left hand Sylvanus and his company: in the way before her, the three Graces, and the three Howres: all of them on everie side wringing their hands, and showeing signe of sorrow for her departure, [and the Poet] being attired as at the first, saving that his cloak was now black, and his garland mixed with ewe branches, to signify sorrow. While she beheld this dumb show, the Poet made her a short oration, as followeth:

The Poet's Speech at her Majestie's Departure
O see, sweet Cynthia, how the wat'ry gods,
Which joyd of late to view thy glorious beames,
At this retire do waile and wring their hands,
Distilling from their eyes salt showrs of teares,
To bring in Winter with their wet lament:
For how can Sommer stay, when Sunne departs?
See where Sylvanus sits, and sadly mournes,
To thinke that Autumn, with his withered wings,
Will bring in tempest, when thy beames are hence:
For how can Sommer stay, when Sunne departs?
See where those Graces, and those Howrs of Heav'n,
Which at thy coming sung triumphal songs,
And smoothd the way, and strewd it with sweet
    flowrs,

---

1. *Nereus:* a sea god; *Sylvane:* forest

Now, if they durst, would stop it with greene bowes,
Lest by thine absence the yeeres pride decay:
For how can Sommer stay, when Sunne departs?
Leaves fal, grasse dies, beasts of the wood hang head,
Birds cease to sing, and everie creature wailes,
To see the season alter with this change:
For how can Sommer stay, when Sunne departs?
O, either stay, or soone returne againe,
For Sommers parting is the countries paine.

Then Nereus, approaching from the ende of the Pond, to hir Majesties coach, on his knees thanked hir Highnesse for hir late largesse, saying as followeth:

Thankes, gracious Goddesse, for they bounteous
   largesse,
Whose worth, although it yields us sweet content,
Yet they depart gives us a greater sorrow.

After this, as her Majestie passd through the parke gate, there was a consort of musicions hidden in a bower; to whose playing this dittie of "Come againe" was sung, with excellent division, by two that were cunning. . . . (As this Song was sung, hir Majestie, notwithstanding the great raine, staied hir coach, and pulled off hir mask, giving great thanks.)

Come againee, faire Nature's treasure,
Whose lookes yeeld joyes exceeding measure.
   [etc. for six couplets]
. . . .
O come againe, sweet beauties Sunne:
When thou art gone, our joyes are done.

Her Majestie was so highly pleased with this and the rest, that she openly said to the Earle of Hertford, that the beginning, processe, and end of this his entertainment, was so honorable, she would not forget the same.

And manie most happie yeares may her gratious Majesty continue, to favour and foster him, and all others which do truly love and honor her.

From The Honorable Entertainment given to the Quene's Majestie, in Progresse, at the Elvetham in Hampshire, by the Right Hon'ble the Earle of Hertford, *1591, ed. John Nichols (1823; New York: AMS Press and Kraus Reprint, 1966).*

11. The Revels Office and Censorship: Keeping It Clean

The master of the revels was originally a court officer, appointed to manage royal entertainments. By Elizabeth's time the office had grown to include oversight of the public theaters, particularly charged with maintaining public order and censoring plays. Many documents of Privy Council proceedings show a high level of anxiety about the theaters. The documents below, for example, chart the appointment of a special commission to regulate players. ✍

A Privy Council Commission to Censor Plays

[1589, Nov. 12. Minute of Privy Council, printed from Register in Dasent, xviii. 214]

At the Starre Chamber 12 Novembris, 1589.

A letter to the Lord Archbishop of Canterbury that whereas there hathe growne some inconvenience by common playes and enterludes in and about the Cyttie of London, in [that] the players take upon themselves to handle in their plaies certen matters of Divinytie and of State unfit to be suffred, for redress whereof their Lordships have thought good to appointe some persones of judgement and understanding to viewe and examine their playes before they be permitted to present them publickly. His Lordship is desired that some fytt persone well learned in Divinity be appointed by him to joyne with the Master of the Revells and one other to be nominated by the Lord Mayour, and they jointly with some spede to viewe and consider suche comedyes and tragedyes as are and shalbe publickly played by the companies of players in and about the Cyttie of London, and they to geve allowance of suche as they shall thincke meete to be plaied and to forbydd the rest.

A letter to the Lord Mayour of London that whereas their Lordships have already signified unto him to appointe a sufficient persone learned and of judgement for the Cyttie of London to joyne with the Master of the Revelles and with a divine to be nominated by the Lord Archebishop of Canterbury for the reforming of the plaies daylie exercised and presented publickly in and about the Cyttie of London, wherein the players take upon them without judgement or decorum to handle matters of Divinitye and State; he is required if he have not as yet made choice of suche a persone, that he will so doe forthwith, and thereof geve knowledge to the Lord Archebishop and the Master of the Revells, that they may all meet accordingly.

A letter to the Master of the Revelles requiring him [to join] with two others the one to be appointed by the Lord Archbishop of Canterbury and the other by the Lord Mayour of London, to be men of learning and judgement, and to call before them the severall companies of players (whose servauntes soever they be) and to require them by authorite hereof to delyver unto them their bookes, that they maye consider of the matters of their comedyes and tragedyes, and thereupon to stryke oute or reforme suche partes and matters as they shall fynd unfytt and undecent to be handled in playes, bothe for Divinitie and State, comaunding the said companies of players, in her Majesties name, that they forbeare to present and playe publickly anie comedy or tragedy other then suche as they three shall have seene and allowed, which if they shall not observe, they shall then knowe from their Lordships that they shalbe not onely sevearely punished, but made incapable of the exercies of their profession forever hereafter.

Competition with Divinity, and with Bear-Baiting

[1591, July 25. Minute of the Privy Council, printed from Register in Dasent, xxi. 324]

A letter to the Lord Maior of the Cyttie of London and the Justices of Midlesex and Surrey. Whereas heretofore there hathe ben order taken to restraine the playinge of enterludes and playes on the Sabothe Daie, notwithsandinge the which (as wee are enformed) the same ys neglected to the prophanacion of this daie, and all other daies of the weeke in divers places the players doe use to recite theire plaies to the greate hurte and destruction of the game of beare baytinge and lyke pastimes, which are maynteyned for her Majesty's pleasure yf occacion require. These shalbe therefore to require you not onlie to take order hereafter that there maie no plaies, interludes or commodyes be used or publicklie made and shewed either on the Sondaie or on the Thursdaies, because on Thursdayes those other games usuallie have ben allwayes accustomed and practized. Whereof see you faile not hereafter to see this our order dulie observed for the avoiydinge of the inconveniences aforesaid.

From The Elizabethan Stage, *vol. 4, ed. E. K. Chambers (Oxford: Clarendon, 1951), 306–7.*

12. A Defense of Plays: From *Pierce Penniless, His Supplication to the Devil* (1592)

In this text, Thomas Nashe (1567–1601), playwright and pamphleteer, defends the theater on the grounds of the positive distraction it provides to an idle populace. The world he describes could use the distraction, because it is caught unhappily between two antagonistic classes of Englishmen: the old, soldierly aristocracy and the rising urban business class. In Nashe's view, the stage resurrects and immortalizes the glory of the "the ancient houses," the traditional nobility whose military prowess and gentlemanly pastimes have made England great. Against these he places the rising merchant class, those "underminers of honor" whose cautious, money-grubbing ways cause "the rust of peace" to dull England's martial might. But Nashe is also interested in the theater as purveyor of historical critique and higher morality, for plays show "the ill success of treason, the fall of hasty climbers, the wretched end of usurpers, the misery of civil dissension, and how just God is evermore in punishing of murther." In making these claims, Nashe sets theater against the self-proclaimed moralists who attack the plays as corrupters of youth. There is also perhaps some

[The Defense of Plays]

That state or kingdom that is in league with all the world, and hath no foreign sword to vex it, is not half so strong or confirmed to endure as that which lives every hour in fear of invasion. There is a certain waste of the people for whom there is no use but war; and these men must have some employment still to cut them off; *Nam si foras hostem non habent, domi invenient.* If they have no service abroad, they will make mutinies at home. Or if the affairs of state be such as cannot exhale all these corrupt excrements, it is very expedient they have some light toys to busy their heads withal, cast before them as bones to gnaw upon, which may keep them from having leisure to intermeddle with higher matters.

To this effect, the policy of plays is very necessary, howsoever some shallow-brained censurers (not the deepest searchers into the secrets of government) mightily oppugn them. For whereas the afternoon being the idlest time of the day, wherein men that are their own masters (as gentlemen of the court, the Inns of the Court, and the number of captains and soldiers about London) do wholly bestow themselves upon pleasure, and that pleasure they divide (how virtuously, it skills not) either into gaming, following of harlots, drinking, or seeing a play; is it not then better (since of four extremes all the world cannot keep them but they will choose one) that they should betake them to the least, which is plays? Nay, what if I prove plays to be no extreme, but a rare exercise of virtue? First, for the subject of them, (for the most part) it is borrowed out of our English chronicles, wherein our forefathers' valiant acts (that have lain long buried in rusty brass and worm-eaten books) are revived, and they themselves raised from the grave of oblivion, and brought to plead their aged honors in open presence; than which, what can be a sharper reproof to these degenerate effeminate days of ours?

How would it have joyed brave Talbot, the terror of the French, to think that after he had lain two hundred years in his tomb, he should triumph again on the stage, and have his bones new embalmed with the tears of ten thousand spectators at least (at several times) who in the tragedian that represents his person imagine they behold him fresh bleeding.

I will defend it against any collian [= rascal] or clubfisted usurer of them all, there is no immortality can be given a man on earth like unto plays. What talk I to them of immortality, that are the only underminers of honor, and do envy any man that is not sprung up by base brokery like themselves. They care not if all the ancient houses were rooted out, so that like the burgomasters of the Low Countries they might share the government amongst them as states, and be quartermasters of our monarchy. All arts to them are vanity; and if you tell them what a glorious thing it is to have Henry the Fifth represented on the stage leading the French king prisoner, and forcing both him and the Dolphin [= Dauphin] to swear fealty, "Aye, but," will they say, "what do we get by it?" Respecting neither the right of fame that is due to true nobility deceased, nor what hopes of eternity are to be proposed to adventurous minds, to encourage them forward, but only their execrable lucre and filthy unquenchable avarice.

They know when they are dead they shall not be brought upon the stage for any goodness, but in a merriment of the usurer and the devil, or buying arms of the herald, who gives them the lion without tongue, tail, or talons, because his master whom he must serve is a townsman and a man of peace, and must not keep any quarreling beasts to annoy his honest neighbors.

In plays, all cozenages [-tricks], all cunning drifts over-gilded with outward holiness, all stratagems of war, all the cankerworms that breed on the rust of peace, are most lively anatomized; they show the ill success of treason, the fall of hasty climbers, the wretched end of usurpers, the misery of civil dissension, and how just God is evermore in punishing of murther. And to prove every one of these allegations could I propound the circumstances of this play and that play, if I meant to handle this theme otherwise than *obiter* [= in passing]. What should I say more? They are sour pills of reprehension wrapped up in sweet words. Whereas some petitioners of the counsel against them object, they corrupt the youth of the city and withdraw prentices from their work; they heartily wish they might be troubled with none of their youth nor their prentices; for some of them (I mean the ruder handicrafts' servants) never come abroad but they are in danger of undoing; and as for corrupting them when they come, that's false; for no play they have encourageth any man to tumults or rebellion, but lays before such the halter and the gallows; or praiseth or approved pride, lust whoredom, prodigality, or drunkenness, but beats them down utterly. As for the hindrance of trades and traders of the city by them, that is an article foisted in by the vintners, alewives, and victualers, who surmise if there were no plays they should have all the company that resort to them lie boozing and beerbathing in their houses every afternoon. Nor so, nor so, good brother bottle ale, for there are other places besides where money can bestow itself; the sign of the smock [i.e., the brothel] will wipe your mouth clean; and yet I have heard ye have made her a tenant to your taphouses. But what shall he do that hath spent himself? Where shall he haunt? Faith, when dice, lust, and drunkenness, and all, have dealt upon him, if there be never a play for him to go to for his penny, he sits melancholy in his chamber, devising upon felony or treason, and how he may best exalt himself by mischief.

13. Classical Comedy for the English Stage: Shakespeare's *Comedy of Errors*

George Puttenham, in The Art of English Poesy *(1589), characterized classical comedy as the earliest form of dramatic poetry, "many voices lively represented to the ear and eye, so as a man might think it were even now a-doing." Accordingly, "the poets devised to have many parts played at once by two or three or four persons that debated the matters of the world—sometimes of their own private affairs, sometimes of their neighbors', but never meddling with any princes' matters, nor such high personages, but commonly of merchants, soldiers, artificers, good honest householders, and also of unthrifty youths, young damsels, old nurses, bawds, brokers, ruffians, and parasites, with such like, in whose behaviors lieth in effect the whole course and trade of man's life." The effect, says Puttenham, was not merely "the good amendment of man by discipline and example" but also "the solace and recreation of the common people, by reason of the pageants and shows."*

England had an ancient tradition of comedy in its morality plays, and in the mid-sixteenth century playwrights began to incorporate the classical forms of Roman comedy. Shakespeare's very early play The Comedy of Errors, *adapted from a comedy of Plautus, relies on devices like mistaken identities and the interplay of hapless servants and their abusive masters. Antipholus, a wealthy gentleman of Syracuse, has come to Ephesus seeking his twin brother (also named Antipholus) and his mother, lost in a sea storm many years before. The lost brother indeed is living, a prosperous married man, in Ephesus, though still unknown to his newly arrived twin. The brothers are served by twin slaves (each named Dromio).*

In the scene that follows, from act 1, scene 2, the newly arrived brother (who is unmarried) has just given his slave a large sum of money to carry safely back to their inn, the Centaur. His brother's slave appears in order to fetch his master home to dinner with his wife. Master and slave each mistake the other for their twin counterparts. Note that the dialogue, though written in well-crafted iambic pentameter, relies on plain, vigorous English rather than high-flown Latinate language. Yet a classical rhetorical form, gradatio, is deployed in Dromio's first speech, where he repeats the last word or phrase of one line ("the meat is cold," etc.) as the first word or phrase of the next. ✍

ANTIPHOLUS OF SYRACUSE
What now? how chance thou art return'd so
    soon?
DROMIO OF EPHESUS
Return'd so soon! rather approach'd too late:
The capon burns, the pig falls from the spit,
The clock hath strucken twelve upon the bell;
My mistress made it one upon my cheek:
She is so hot because the meat is cold;
The meat is cold because you come not home;
You come not home because you have no stomach;
You have no stomach having broke your fast;
But we that know what 'tis to fast and pray
Are penitent for your default to-day.
ANTIPHOLUS OF SYRACUSE
Stop in your wind, sir: tell me this, I pray:
Where have you left the money that I gave you?
DROMIO OF EPHESUS
O,—sixpence, that I had o' Wednesday last
To pay the saddler for my mistress' crupper?
The saddler had it, sir; I kept it not.
ANTIPHOLUS OF SYRACUSE
I am not in a sportive humour now:
Tell me, and dally not, where is the money?
We being strangers here, how darest thou trust
So great a charge from thine own custody?
DROMIO OF EPHESUS
I pray you, sir, as you sit at dinner:
I from my mistress come to you in post;
If I return, I shall be post indeed,
For she will score your fault upon my pate.
Methinks your maw, like mine, should be your
    clock,

And strike you home without a messenger.
ANTIPHOLUS OF SYRACUSE
Come, Dromio, come, these jests are out of season;
Reserve them till a merrier hour than this.
Where is the gold I gave in charge to thee?
DROMIO OF EPHESUS
To me, sir? why, you gave no gold to me.
ANTIPHOLUS OF SYRACUSE
Come on, sir knave, have done your foolishness,
And tell me how thou hast disposed thy charge.
DROMIO OF EPHESUS
My charge was but to fetch you from the mart
Home to your house, the Phoenix,[1] sir, to dinner:
My mistress and her sister stays for you.
ANTIPHOLUS OF SYRACUSE
In what safe place you have bestow'd my money,
Or I shall break that merry sconce of yours
That stands on tricks when I am undisposed:
Where is the thousand marks thou hadst of me?
DROMIO OF EPHESUS
I have some marks of yours upon my pate,
Some of my mistress' marks upon my shoulders,
But not a thousand marks between you both.
If I should pay your worship those again,
Perchance you will not bear them patiently.
ANTIPHOLUS OF SYRACUSE
Thy mistress' marks? What mistress, slave, hast
    thou?
DROMIO OF EPHESUS
Your worship's wife, my mistress at the Phoenix;
She that doth fast till you come home to dinner,
And prays that you will hie you home to dinner.
ANTIPHOLUS OF SYRACUSE
What, wilt thou flout me thus unto my face,
Being forbid? There, take you that, sir knave.
DROMIO OF EPHESUS
What mean you, sir? for God's sake, hold your hands!
Nay, and you will not, sir, I'll take my heels.
        Exit
ANTIPHOLUS OF SYRACUSE
Upon my life, by some device or other
The villain is o'er-raught of all my money.

1. the Phoenix: an inn

They say this town is full of cozenage,[1]
As, nimble jugglers[2] that deceive the eye,
Dark-working sorcerers that change the mind,
Soul-killing witches that deform the body,
Disguised cheaters, prating mountebanks,[3]
And many such-like liberties of sin:
If it prove so, I will be gone the sooner.
I'll to the Centaur, to go seek this slave:
I greatly fear my money is not safe.

     Exit

14. Classical Tragedy for the English Stage: Kyd's *Spanish Tragedie* (ca. 1589)

George Puttenham, in The Art of English Poesy *(1589), extolled classical tragedy as the form of poetry in which "the evil and outrageous behaviors of princes were reprehended . . . their infamous life and tyrannies were laid open to all the world, their wickedness reproached, their follies and extreme insolencies derided, and their miserable ends painted out in plays and pageants to show the mutability of fortune and the just punishment of God in revenge of a vicious and evil life."*

Thomas Kyd's The Spanish Tragedy, *as the scene below illustrates, brings arrogant princes to a grisly end. Kyd employs the conventions of Greek and Roman tragedy, including noble characters, stately verse, finely wrought rhetoric, and high passions. But he added to his classical models certain elements familiar to English audiences from their traditional popular drama: sensational (even gross) onstage incidents and fabulous spectacles. Kyd's play was one of the most popular plays of the 1590s, and showed that English poets were ready to forge a new kind of drama for the London stage. It set the fashion for the tragedy of revenge that deeply influenced Marlowe, Shakespeare, and other playwrights. This scene employs the device of the play-within-a-play, and in doing so reflects on the uses of drama to purge folly and evil.*

1. *cozenage:* fraud
2. *jugglers:* swindlers
3. *mountebanks:* charlatans

In the scene (act 4, scene 1), a nobleman of Spain, **Hieronimo**, *whose son has been murdered by the princes* **Balthazar** *and* **Lorenzo**, *conspires with his son's beloved,* **Bel Imperia**, *to avenge the killing by means of a play to be staged for the king, during which the princes, playing parts in the tragedy, will themselves be killed.* ✆

BEL IMPERIA: Hieronimo, I will consent, conceale,
And ought that may effect for thine availe,[1]
Joyne with thee to revenge Horatio's death.
HIERONIMO: On then, [and] whatsoever I devise,
Let me entreat you grace my practice,[2]
For-why[3] the plots already in mine head.—
Heere they are!
    Enter BALTHAZAR and LORENZO.
BALTHAZAR: How now, Hieronimo?
What, courting Bel-imperia?
HIERONIMO: Aye, my lord,
Such courting as, I promise you,
She hath my hart, but you, my lord, have hers.
LORENZO: But now, Hieronimo, or never
we are to intreate your helpe.
HIERONIMO: My help?
Why, my good lords, assure your-selves of me;
For you have given me cause,—Aye, by my faith,
   have you!
BALTHAZAR: It pleasde you at the entertainment of
   the ambassadour,
To grace the King so much as with a shew;
Now were your study so well furnished
As, for the passing of the first nights sport,
To entertaine my father with the like,
Or any such like pleasing motion,
Assure yourselfe it would content them well.
HIERONIMO: Is this all?
BALTHAZAR: Aye, this is all.
HIERONIMO: Why then ile fit[4] you; say no more.
When I was yong I gave my minde
And plide my-selfe to fruitles poetrie,

1. "and anything that may help your benefit"
2. *practice:* scheme
3. *For-why:* why
4. fit: please

Which, though it profite the professor naught,
Yet is it passing[1] pleasing to the world.
LORENZO: And how for that?
HIERONIMO: Marrie, my good lord, thus.
—And yet, me thinks, you are too quick with us!—
When in Tolledo there I studied,
It was my chaunce to write a tragedie,—
See heere, my lords,

     He showes them a book.

Which, long forgot, I found this other day.
Nor would your lordships favour me so much
As but to grace me with your acting it,
I meane each one of you to play a part.
Assure you it will proue most passing strange[2]
And wondrous plausible to that assembly.
BALTHAZAR: What, would you have us play a
    tragedie?
HIERONIMO: Why, Nero thought it no disparage-
    ment,
And kings and emperours have ta'en delight
To make experience of their wit in plaies!
LORENZO: Nay, be not angry, good Hieronimo;
The prince but asked a question.
BALTHAZAR: In faith, Hieronimo, and you be in
    earnest,
I'll make one.[3]
LORENZO: And I another.
HIERONIMO: Now, my good lord, could you intreat,
Your sister, Bel-imperia, to make one,—
For what's a play without a woman in it?
BEL IMPERIA: Little intreaty shall serve me,
    Hieronimo,
For I must needs be imployed in your play.
HIERONIMO: Why, this is well! I tell you, lordings,
It was determined to have beene acted,
By gentlemen and schollers too,
Such as could tell what to speak.
BALTHAZAR: And now it shall be plaide by princes
    and courtiers,
Such as can tell how to speak,
If, as it is our country manner,

1. passing: extremely
2. strange: wonderful, exotic
3. *make one:* join in, play a part

You will but let us know the argument.[1]
HIERONIMO: That shall I roundly. The cronicles of
    Spaine
Recorde this written of a knight of Rhodes;
He was betrothed, and wedded at the length,
To one Perseda, an Italian dame,
Whose beautie ravished all that her behelde,
Especially the soule of Soliman,
Who at the marriage was the cheefest guest.
By sundry meanes sought Soliman to winne
Persedas love, and could not gaine the same.
Then gan he break his passions to a freend,
One of his bashawes[2] whome he held full deere.
Her has this bashaw long solicited,
And saw she was not otherwise to be wonne
But by her husband's death, this knight of Rhodes,
Whome presently by trecherie his slew.
She, stirde with an exceeding hate therefore,
As cause of this, slew [Sultan] Soliman,
And, to escape the bashawe's tirannie,
Did stab her-selfe. And this [is] the tragedie.
LORENZO: O, excellent!
BEL IMPERIA: But say, Hieronimo:
What then became of him that was the bashaw?
HIERONIMO: Marrie thus: moved with remorse of
    his misdeeds,
Ran to a mountain top and hung himselfe.
BALTHAZAR: But which of us is to performe that part?
HIERONIMO: O, that will I, my lords; make no
    doubt of it;
Ile play the murderer, I warrant you;
For I already have conceited[3] that
BALTHAZAR: And what shall I?
HIERONIMO: Great Soliman, the Turkish emperour.
LORENZO: And I?
HIERONIMO: Erastus, the knight of Rhodes.
BEL IMPERIA: And I?
HIERONIMO: Perseda, chaste and resolute.
And heere, my lords, are several abstracts drawne,
For eache of you to note your [severall] partes.

1. argument: plot
2. *bashawes:* dignitaries
3. conceited: imagined, plotted

And act it as occasion's offred you.
You must provide [you with] a Turkish cappe,
A black moustache and a fauchion.
    Gives paper to BAL[THAZAR].
You with a crosse, like a knight of Rhodes.
    Gives another to LOR[ENZO].
And, madame, you must [then] attire your-selfe
    He giveth BEL[-IMPERIA] another.
Like Phoebe, Flora, or the huntresse [Dian],
Which to your discretion shall seeme best.
And as for me, my lords, Ile looke to one,
And with the raunsome that the viceroy sent
So furnish and performe this tragedie
As all the world shall say Hieronimo
Was liberall in gracing of it so.
BALTHAZAR: Hieronimo, methinks a comedie
    were better.
HIERONIMO: A comedie? fie! comedies are fit for
    common wits;
But to present a kingly troupe withall,
Give me a stately-written tragedie,—
Tragedia cothurnata,[1] fitting kings,
Containing matter, and not common things!
My lords, all this [our sport] must be perfourmed,
As fitting, for the first night's revelling.
The Italian tragedians were so sharpe
Of wit that in one houre's meditation
They would performe any-thing in action.
LORENZO: And well it may, for I have seene the
    like
In Paris, mongst the French tragedians.
HIERONIMO: In Paris? Mass, and well remembered!—
There's one thing more that rests for us to do.
BALTHAZAR: What's that, Hieronimo? Forget not
    anything.
HIERONIMO: Each one of us must act his parte
In vnknowne languages,
That it may breede the more varietie:
As you, my lord, in Latin, I in Greeke,
You in Italian, and, for-because I know
That Bel-imperia hath practised the French,
In courtly French shall all her phrases be.

1. *Tragedia cothurnata:* lofty tragedy

BEL IMPERIA: You meane to try my cunning then,
    Hieronimo!
BALTHAZAR: But this will be a meere[1] confusion,
And hardly shall we all be vnderstoode.
HIERONIMO: It must be so; for the conclusion
Shall prove the invention and all was good;
And I my-selfe in an oration,
That I will have there behinde a curtaine,
And with a strange and wondrous shew besides,
Assure yourselfe, shall make the matter knowne.
And all shalbe concluded in once scene,
For there's no pleasure taken in tediousness.
BALTHAZAR: [to LORENZO] How like you this?
LORENZO: Why thus, my lord, we must resolve,
To soothe his humors up.[2]
HIERONIMO: You'll plie this geere?[3]
LORENZO: I warrant you.
    Exeuent[4] all but HIERONIMO.
HIERONIMO: Why, so! now shall I see the fall of
    Babylon
Wrought by the heavens in this confusion.
And, if the world like not this tragedie,
Hard is the hap[5] of olde Hieronimo.
    Exit.

15. Aristotle on Drama

*Shakespeare and Marlowe probably had no direct
knowledge of Aristotle's theories of poetic art. Even
so, his ideas on the innate pleasures of representation, the relation of history to poetry, and the
elements of tragedy (especially the "tragic flaw")
have shaped critical observations on the Elizabethan dramatists for centuries. These observations
can also be deployed in creative defense or indictment of the authors in the contest. On one hand, the
English playwrights seem to follow Aristotle's rules
when they interpret their historical sources loosely
for dramatic (or political) effect. So, too, they mix
plot and "song." On the other hand, they depart*

1. *meere:* complete, total
2. *soothe his humors up:* pacify him
3. *plie this geere:* put on these clothes
4. Exeuent: two or more characters leave the stage
5. *hap:* luck, fortune

wildly from Aristotle's rules of unified action, and they mix "high" and "low" elements freely. ☙

Speaking generally, poetry seems to owe its origin to two particular causes, both natural. From childhood men have an instinct for representation, and in this respect, differs from the other animals that he is far more imitative and learns his first lessons by representing things. And then there is the enjoyment people always get from representations. What happens in actual experience proves this, for we enjoy looking at accurate likenesses of things which are themselves painful to see, obscene beasts, for instance, and corpses. The reason is this: Learning things gives great pleasure not only to philosophers but also in the same way to all other men, though they share this pleasure only to a small degree. The reason why we enjoy seeing likenesses is that, as we look, we learn and infer what each is, for instance, "that is so and so." If we have never happened to see the original, our pleasure is not due to the representation as such but to the technique or the color or some other such cause.

We have, then, a natural instinct for representation and for tune and rhythm—for the metres are obviously sections of rhythms—and starting with these instincts men very gradually developed them until they produced poetry out of their improvisations. Poetry then split into two kinds according to the poet's nature. For the more serious poets represented fine doings and the doings of fine men, while those of a less exalted nature represented the actions of inferior men, at first writing satire just as the others at first wrote hymns and eulogies. . . . When tragedy and comedy came to light, poets were drawn by their natural bent towards one or the other. Some became writers of comedies instead of lampoons, the others produced tragedies instead of epics; the reason being that the former is in each case a higher kind of art and has greater value.

. . . Comedy, as we have said, is a representation of inferior people, not indeed in the full sense of the word bad, but the laughable is a species of the base or ugly. It consists in some blunder or ugliness that does not cause pain or disaster, an obvious example being the comic mask which is ugly and distorted but not painful.

. . . Tragedy is, then, a representation of an action that is heroic and complete and of a certain magnitude—by means of language enriched with all kinds of ornament, each used separately in the different parts of the play: it represents men in action and does not use narrative, and through pity and fear it effects relief to these and similar emotions. By "language enriched" I mean that which has rhythm and tune, i.e., song, and by "the kinds separately" I mean that some effects are produced by verse alone and some again by song.

Since the representation is performed by living persons, it follows at once that one essential part of a tragedy is the spectacular effect, and, besides that, song-making and diction. For these are the means of the representation. By "diction" I mean here the metrical arrangement of the words; and "song making" I use in the full, obvious sense of the word. And since tragedy represents action and is acted by living persons, who must of necessity have certain qualities of character and thought—for it is these which determine the quality of an action; indeed thought and character are the natural causes of any action and it is in virtue of these that all men succeed or fail—it follows then that it is the plot which represents the action. By "plot" I mean here the arrangement of the incidents: "character" is that which determines the quality of the agents, and "thought" appears wherever in the dialogue they put forward an argument or deliver an opinion.

Necessarily then every tragedy has six constituent parts, and on these its quality depends. These are plot, character, diction, thought, spectacle, and song. Two of these are the means of representation: one is the manner: three are the objects represented. This list is exhaustive, and practically all the poets employ these elements, for every drama includes alike spectacle and character and plot and diction and song and thought.

The most important of these is the arrangement of the incidents, for tragedy is not a representation of men but of a piece of action, of life, of happiness and unhappiness, which come under the head of action, and the end aimed at is the representation not of qualities of character but of some action; and while character makes men what they are, it's their actions and experiences that make them happy or the opposite. They do not therefore act to represent character, but character-study is included for the sake of the action. It follows that the incidents and the plot are the end at which tragedy aims, and in everything the end aimed at is of prime importance. Moreover, you could not have a tragedy without action, but you can have one without character-study. . . .

The plot then is the first principle and as it were the soul of tragedy: character comes second. It is much the same also in painting; if a man smeared a canvas with the loveliest colors at random, it would not give as much pleasure as an outline in black and white. And it is mainly because a play is a representation of action that it also for that reason represents people. . . .

Character is that which reveals choice, shows what sort of thing a man chooses or avoids in circumstances where the choice is not obvious, so those speeches convey no character in which there is nothing whatever which the speaker chooses or avoids.

Of the other elements which "enrich" tragedy the most important is song-making. Spectacle, while highly effective, is yet quite foreign to the art and has nothing to do with poetry. Indeed the effect of tragedy does not depend on its performance by actors, and, moreover, for achieving the spectacular effects the art of the costumier is more authoritative than that of the poet.

After these definitions we must next discuss the proper arrangement of the incidents since this is the first and most important thing in tragedy. We have laid it down that tragedy is a representation of an action that is whole and complete and of a certain magnitude, since a thing may be a whole and yet have no magnitude. A whole is what has a

beginning and middle and end. A beginning is that which is not a necessary consequent of anything else but after which something else exists or happens as a natural result. An end on the contrary is that which is inevitably or, as a rule, the natural result of something else but from which nothing else follows; a middle follows something else and something follows from it. Well constructed plots must not therefore begin and end at random, but must embody the formulae we have stated.

. . . What we have said already makes it further clear that a poet's object is not to tell what actually happened but what could and would happen either probably or inevitably. The difference between a historian and a poet is not that one writes in prose and the other in verse—indeed the writings of Herodotus could be put into verse and yet would still be a kind of history, whether written in metre or not. The real difference is this, that one tells what happened and the other what might happen. For this reason poetry is something more scientific and serious than history, because poetry tends to give general truths while history gives particular facts.

By a "general truth" I mean the sort of thing that a certain type of man will do or say either probably or necessarily. That is what poetry aims at in giving names to the characters. A "particular fact" is what Alcibiades did or what was done to him. In the case of comedy this has now become obvious, for comedians construct their plots out of probable incidents and then put in any names that occur to them. They do not, like the iambic satirists, write about individuals. In tragedy, on the other hand, they keep to real names. The reason is that what is possible carries conviction. If a thing has not happened, we do not yet believe in its possibility, but what has happened is obviously possible. Had it been impossible, it would not have happened. . . . One need not therefore endeavor invariably to keep to the traditional stories with which our tragedies deal. Indeed it would be absurd to do that, seeing that the familiar themes are familiar only to a few and yet please all.

It is clear, then, from what we have said that the poet must be a "maker" not of verses but of stories, since he is a poet in virtue of his "representation," and what he represents is action. Even supposing he represents what has actually happened, he is none the less a poet, for there is nothing to prevent some actual occurrences being the sort of thing that would probably or inevitably happen, and it is in virtue of that that he is their "maker."

Of "simple" plots and actions the worst are those which are "episodic." By this I mean a plot in which the episodes do not follow each other probably or inevitably. Bad poets write such plays because they cannot help it, and good poets write them to please the actors. Writing as they do for competition, they often strain a plot beyond its capacity and are thus obliged to sacrifice continuity. But this is bad work, since tragedy represents not only a complete action but also incidents that cause fear and pity, and this happens most of all when the incidents are unexpected and yet one is a consequence of the other. For in that way the incidents will cause more amazement than if they happened mechanically and accidentally, since the most amazing accidental occurrences are those which seem to have been providential. . . . Such events do not seem to be mere accidents. So such plots as these must necessarily be the best.

Some plots are "simple" and some "complex," as indeed the actions represented by the plots are obviously such. By a simple action I mean one that is single and continuous in the sense of our definition above, wherein the change of fortune occurs without "reversal" or "discovery"; by a complex action I mean one wherein the change coincides with a "discovery" or "reversal" or both. These should result from the actual structure of the plot in such a way that what has already happened makes the result inevitable or probable; for there is indeed a vast difference between what happens propter hoc and post hoc.

A "reversal" is a change of the situation into the opposite, as described above, this change being, moreover, as we are saying, probable or inevitable—like the man in the *Oedipus* who came to cheer Oedipus and rid him of his anxiety about his mother by revealing his parentage and changed the whole situation. . . .

A "discovery," as the term itself implies, is a change from ignorance to knowledge, producing either friendship or hatred in those who are destined for good fortune or ill. A discovery is most effective when it coincides with reversals, such as that involved by the discovery in the *Oedipus*. There are also other forms of discovery, for what we have described may in a sense occur in relation to inanimate and trivial objects, or one may discover whether some one has done something or not. But the discovery which is most essentially part of the plot and part of the action is of the kind described above, for such a discovery and reversal of fortune will involve either pity or fear. Nor again the passing of a thoroughly bad man from good fortune to bad fortune. Such a structure might satisfy our feelings but it arouses neither pity nor fear, the one being for the man who does not deserve his misfortune and the other for the man who is like ourselves—pity for the undeserved misfortune, fear for the man like ourselves—so that the result will arouse neither pity nor fear.

There remains then the mean between these. This is the sort of man who is not pre-eminently virtuous and just, and yet it is through no badness or villainy of his own that he falls into the fortune, but rather through some flaw in him,[1] he being one of those who are in high station and good fortune, like Oedipus and Thyestes and the famous men of

---

1. *Translator's note:* Whether Aristotle regards the "flaw" as intellectual or moral has been hotly discussed. It may cover both senses. The hero must not deserve his misfortune, but he must cause it by making a fatal mistake, an error of judgement, which may well involve some imperfection of character but not such as to make us regard him as "morally responsible" for the disasters although they are nevertheless the consequences of the flaw in him, and his wrong decision at a crisis is the inevitable outcome of his character. [It must be noted as well that the hero's "flaw" is often the outgrowth of his or her primary virtue, as when great courage tends to rashness, or keen intelligence to restlessness or overthinking.]

such families as those. The successful plot must then have a single and not, as some say, a double issue; and the change must be not to good fortune from bad but, on the contrary, from good to bad fortune, and it must not be due to villainy but to some great flaw in such a man as we have described, or of one who is better rather than worse. This can be seen also in actual practice.

. . . Fear and pity sometimes result from the spectacle and are sometimes aroused by the actual arrangement of the incidents, which is preferable and the mark of a better poet. The plot should be so constructed that even without seeing the play anyone hearing of the incidents happening thrills with fear and pity as a result of what occurs. So would anyone feel who heard the story of Oedipus. To produce this effect by means of an appeal to the eye is inartistic and needs adventitious aid, while those who by such means produce an effect which is not fearful but merely monstrous have nothing in common with tragedy. For one should not seek from tragedy all kinds of pleasure but that which is peculiar to tragedy, and since the poet must by "representation" produce the pleasure which comes from feeling pity and fear, obviously this quality must be embodied in the incidents.

We must now decide what incidents seem dreadful or rather pitiable. Such must necessarily be the actions of friends to each other or of enemies or of people that are neither. Now if an enemy does it to an enemy, there is nothing pitiable either in the deed or the intention, except so far as the actual calamity goes. Nor would there be if they were neither friends nor enemies. But when these calamities happen among friends, when for instance brother kills brother, or son father, or mother son, or son mother—either kills or intends to kill, or does something of the kind, that is what we must look for.

From The Poetics, *translated by W. H. Fyfe (1927)*

16. Sidney on Drama:
The Defense of Poetry (1579?)

Sir Philip Sidney (1554–86) has often been held up as the prime example of the Elizabethan courtier:

soldier, scholar, poet, he died heroically on the battlefield at an early age, leaving nonetheless an impressive body of writing. Playing on a classical theme (compare Aristotle's Poetics), Sidney asserts in his Defense of Poetry the superiority of poetry over history and philosophy as a way of advancing humanist ideals. Though elsewhere he sees gross faults in English drama, he argues here for the value both of comedy and of tragedy for purging folly and evil. ☙

No, perchance it is the comic [that critics of poetry despise]; whom naughty[1] play-makers and stage-keepers have justly made odious. To the argument of abuse I will answer after. Only thus much now is to be said, that the comedy is an imitation of the common errors of our life, which he representeth in the most ridiculous and scornful sort that may be, so as it is impossible that any beholder can be content to be such a one. Now, as in geometry the oblique must be known as well as the right, and in arithmetic the odd as well as the even; so in the actions of our life who seeth not the filthiness of evil, wanteth a great foil to perceive the beauty of virtue. This doth the comedy handle so, in our private and domestical matters, as with hearing it we get, as it were, an experience what is to be looked for of a niggardly Demea, of a crafty Davus, of a flattering Gnatho, of a vain-glorious Thraso;[2] and not only to know what effects are to be expected, but to know who be such, by the signifying badge given them by the comedian. And little reason hath any man to say that men learn evil by seeing it so set out, since, as I said before, there is no man living, but by the force truth hath in nature, no sooner seeth these men play their parts, but wisheth them in pistrinum,[3] although perchance the sack of his own faults lie so behind his back, that he seeth not himself to dance the same measure,—whereto yet nothing can more open his eyes than to find his own actions contemptibly set

1. naughty: wicked
2. all type-characters in classical comedy
3. condemned to servitude at the mill-wheel

forth. So that the right use of comedy will, I think, by nobody be blamed, and much less of the high and excellent tragedy, that openeth the greatest wounds, and showeth forth the ulcers that are covered with tissue; that maketh kings fear to be tyrants, and tyrants manifest their tyrannical humors; that with stirring the effects of admiration and commiseration teacheth the uncertainty of this world, and upon how weak foundations gilden roofs are builded; that maketh us know:

Qui sceptra saevus duro imperio regit,
Timet timentes, metus in auctorem redit

[The cruel master who rules with harsh command Fears the fearful; terror returns to its author.]

But how much it can move, Plutarch yieldeth a notable testimony of the abominable tyrant Alexander Phéraeus, from whose eyes a tragedy, well made and represented, drew abundance of tears, who without all pity had murdered infinite numbers, and some of his own blood; so as he that was not ashamed to make matters for tragedies, yet could not resist the sweet violence of a tragedy. And if it wrought no further good in him, it was that he, in despite of himself, withdrew himself from hearkening to that which might mollify his hardened heart. But it is not the tragedy they do mislike, for it were too absurd to cast out so excellent a representation of whatsoever is most worthy to be learned.

DOCUMENTS OF THE KINGDOM AND ITS CHURCH

What mighty conflicts of church and state may echo in the conflicts of our stage?

17. The Tudor Succession: From Raphael Holinshed's *Chronicles* (1587)

When Elizabeth's grandfather, Henry VII, seized the English throne in 1485, his people could hope that a century of dynastic violence (the so-called Wars of the Roses) had come to an end. Indeed, the early decades of Tudor rule showed progress toward

stabilization, and the young Henry VIII was crowned in 1509 amid predictions of a new golden age of peace, prosperity, and learning. When the early rumblings of the Lutheran Reformation began to shake Europe, the young king of England published a spirited defense of the Catholic faith and was rewarded by the pope. Yet Henry's own early dynastic worries—he had no son until 1537 (Edward VI)—soon drove him and all England into religious and political turmoil that shaped the reigns of his three children, Edward, Mary, and Elizabeth, to the end of the sixteenth century and far beyond. ✄

1521: The Young King Henry VIII Declared Defender of the Faith by the Pope, as Reward for Henry's Attack on Luther

On the second daie of Februarie, the king as then being at Greenewich, receiued a bull [= decree] from the pope, whereby he was declared Defendor of the Christian faith & likewise his successors for euer. The cardinall of Yorke sang the high masse that daie with all the pompous solemnitie that might be, and gaue cleane remission of sinnes to all that heard it. This title was ascribed vnto the king, bicause he had written a booke against Luther in Germanie; wherevnto the said Luther answered verie sharpelie, nothing sparing his authoritie nor maiestie. Of which booke published by the king, I will not (for reuerence of his roialtie) though I durst, report what I haue read: bicause we are to iudge honourablie of our rulers, and to speake nothing but good of the princes of the people. Onelie this breefe clause or fragment I will adde (least I might seeme to tell a tale of the man in the moone) that king Henrie in his said booke is reported to rage against the diuell and antichrist, to cast out his some [?] against Luther, to rase out the name of the pope, and yet to allow his law, &c. I suppresse the rest for shame, and returne to our historie.

1533: Princess Elizabeth Born (Four Months after Her Father Marries Her Mother)

The seuenth of September being sundaie, betweene three & foure of the clocke in the afternoone, the queene was deliuered of a faire yoong ladie, on which daie the duke of Norffolke came home to the christening, which was appointed on the wednesdaie next following, and was accordinglie accomplished on the same daie, with all such solemne ceremonies as were thought conuenient. The godfather at the font, was the lord archbishop of Canturburie, the godmothers, the old dutches of Norffolke, & the old marchionesse Dorset widow and at the confirmation the ladie marchionesse of Excester was godmother: the child was named Elizabeth.

1534: Monasteries Suppressed and Henry Declared Supreme Head of the Church of England

The eleuenth of August were all the places of the obseruant friers suppressed, as Greenwich, Canturburie, Richmont, Newarke, and Newcastell, and in their places were set Augustine friers, and the obseruant friers were placed in the roomes of the graie friers. The one and twentith of September, doctor Tailor master of the rolles, was discharged of that office, and Thomas Cromwell sworne in his place the ninteenth of October. Moreouer the third of Nouember, the parlement began againe, in the which was concluded the act of supremacie, which authorised the kings highnes to be supreme head of the church of England, and the authoritie of the pope abolished out of the realme. In the same parlement also was giuen to the king, the first fruits and tenths of all spirituall dignities and promotions.

1536: Queen Anne (Mother of Queen Elizabeth) Tried and Beheaded

On the fifteenth of Maie queene Anne was arreigned in the tower of London on a scaffold for that purpose, made in the kings hall, before the duke of Norffolke, who sate vnder the cloth of estate as high steward of England, with the lord chancellor on his right hand, the duke of Suffolke on his left hand, with marquesses and lords, &c: and the earle of Surrie sat before the duke of Norffolke his father, as earle marshall of England. The kings commission being read, the constable of the tower, and the lieutenant brought the queene to the barre, where was made a chaire for her to sit downe in, and there her indictement was read, wherevnto she made so wise and discreet answers, that she seemed fullie to cleere her selfe of all matters laid to her charge: but being tried by her peeres, whereof the duke of Suffolke was chiefe, she was by them found guiltie, and had iudgement pronounced by the duke of Norffolke.

On the nineteenth of Maie queene Anne was on a scaffold (made for that purpose) vpon the greene within the tower of London, beheaded with the sword of Calis, by the hands of the hangman of that towne: her bodie with the head was buried in the queere[1] of the chappell in the tower.

At Henry VIII's Death, Edward VI, the Boy King, Moves toward a More Protestant Church of England

Also shortlie after his coronation, the kings maiestie by the aduise of his vncle the lord protector [Somerset] and other of his priuie councell, minding first of all to seeke Gods honor and glorie, and therevpon intending a reformation, did not onelie set foorth by certeine commissioners, sundrie iniunctions for the remoouing of images out of all churches, to the suppressing and auoiding of idolatrie and superstition within his realmes and dominions, but also caused certeine homilies or sermons to be drawne by sundrie godlie & learned men, that the same might be read in churches to the people, which were afterward by certeine of these commissioners sent foorth as visitors, accompanied with certeine preachers throughout the realme, for the better instruction of the people, published and put in vse. At Easter next following, he set out also an order thorough all the realme, that the supper of the lord should be ministred to the laie people in both kinds [both the wine and the bread, in contrast to Roman Catholic practice, which administered only the bread to lay communicants].

1. queere: the chancel, or part of the church where the quoir sings

After Edward's Death and an Attempt by Protestants to Crown Lady Jane Grey in 1553, Mary Tudor Accedes, Restores England to the Roman Catholic Religion

After that quéene Marie was thus with full consent of the nobles and commons of the realme proclamed queene, she being then in Northfolke, at her castell of Framingham, repaired with all speed to the citie of London: and the third daie of the said moneth of August she came to the said citie, and so to the tower, where the ladie Iane of Suffolke (late afore proc-lamed queene) with her husband the lord Gilford, a little before her comming, were committed to ward, & there remained almost after fiue moneths. And by the waie, as the quéene thus passed, she was ioifullie saluted of all the people, without anie misliking; sauing that it was much feared of manie, that she would alter the religion set foorth by king Edward her brother, whereof then were giuen iust occasions: because (notwithstanding diuerse lawes made to the contrarie) she had dailie masse and Latine seruice said before her in the tower. Yea it was doubted in like sort, that she would both adnull and innouat certeine lawes and decrees established by the yoong prince her predecessor.

Soon Mary Beheads Edward's Chief Protestant Advisers, Somerset and Northumberland, Who Are Buried in the Tower, Near Two of Henry VIII's Beheaded Wives

On the two and twentith of August Iohn duke of Northumberland was beheaded on the tower hill, whose bodie with the head was buried in the tower, by the bodie of Edward late duke of Sumerset. So that there lieth before the high altar two dukes betweene two queenes, to wit, the duke of Summerset & the duke of Northumberland betweene queene Anne [Boleyn, mother of Elizabeth] and queene Katharine [Howard, Henry VIII's fifth wife], all foure beheaded.

Mary Marries Philip, the Catholic King of Spain, and Restores Catholicism in England

Then would she needs bring in king Philip, and by her strange marriage with him, make the whole realme of England subiect vnto a stranger. And all that notwithstanding, either that she did or was able to doo, she could not bring to passe to set the crowne of England vpon his head. With king Philip also came in the pope and his popish masse: with whome also her purpose was to restore againe the monks and nunnes vnto their places, neither lacked there all kind of attempts to the vttermost of her abilitie: and yet therein also God stopt her of her will, that it came not forward. After this, what a dearth happened in her time here in her land, the like wherof hath not lightlie in England beene seene, in so much that in sundrie places her poore subiects were fame [starved] to feed of acorns for want of corne.

1558: On Mary's Death, Elizabeth Comes to the Throne

THE PRAIER OF QUEENE ELISABETH AS SHE WENT TO HER CORONATION.

O Lord almightie and euerlasting God, I giue thee most hartie thanks, that thou hast beene so mercifull vnto me, as to spare me to behold this ioifull daie. And I acknowledge that thou hast delt as woonderfullie and as mercifullie with me, as thou diddest with thy true and faithfull seruant Daniell thy prophet; whome thou deliueredst out of the den from the crueltie of the greedie and raging lions: euen so was I ouerwhelmed, and onlie by thee deliuered. To thee therefore onlie be thankes, honor, and praise, for euer:
Amen.

18. Via Media: The Elizabethan Settlement of Religion, from Raphael Holinshed's *Chronicles* (1587)

Throughout the sixteenth century (and long after) English Christians fought over the relationship between organized religion and individual faith. The Roman Catholic tradition held that salvation lay only through the church and its ordained priests, while Protestants argued for salvation through a more direct relationship between each believer and holy scripture. The conflict between these two views rose from centuries of abuse and neglect by church authorities, and from the ideas of Martin Luther and then John Calvin. Elizabeth's father, Henry VIII, used the cause of church reform to advance his own dynastic ambitions, including his wish to divorce and remarry in order to produce a male heir. Such a divorce was prohibited in the Catholic dispensation. King Henry broke from Rome and formed the Church of England in 1534, the year after Elizabeth's birth. Over the ensuing decades factions of radical and moderate Protestants and loyal Roman Catholics fought (and killed) for control of the English church. Before Elizabeth came to the throne in 1558, the Roman Catholic communion had been restored in England by her sister Mary. At the same time a rising Puritan minority agitated for control of the English church. Elizabeth, guided by moderate theologians, instituted a via media, *or "middle way," by which English Christians might be guided both by Catholic tradition and by reformed principles of scriptural purity. ✆*

The Newly Crowned Queen Elizabeth Restores the Church of England to Some Reformed Practices

The thirteenth of December being tuesdaie, the corps of queene Marie was right honorablie conueied from her manor of S. Iames, vnto the abbeie of Westminster. Her picture was laid on the coffin, apparelled in her roiall robes, with a crowne of gold set on the head thereof, after a solemne manner.

On sundaie the first of Ianuarie, by vertue of the queenes proclamation, the English letanie was read accordinglie as was vsed in her graces chappell in churches through the citie of London. And likewise the epistle and gospell of the daie began to be read in the same churches at masse time in the English tongue, by commandement giuen by the lord maior, according to the tenour of the same proclamation, published the thirtith of the last month.

1558: Early in Her Reign Elizabeth Calls a Church Council to Work Out a Settlement

The last of March the parlement yet continuing, was a conference begun at Westminster concerning certeine articles of religion betwixt the bishops and other of the clergie on the one part, and certeine learned preachers of whome some had beene in dignitie in the church of England before that time on the other part. The declaration of the proceeding wherin, and the cause of the breaking vp of the same conference by default and contempt of certeine bishops, parties of the said conference was published in a little treatise, and imprinted by Richard Iug and Iohn Cawood, printers to the queenes maiestie, as here followeth. The queenes most excellent maiestie, hauing heard of diuersitie of opinions in certeine matters of religion amongst sundrie of her louing subiects, and being verie desirous to haue the same reduced to some godlie & christian concord, thought it best by the aduise of the lords, and other of her priuie councell, as well for the satisfaction of persons doubtfull, as also for the knowlege of the verie truth in certeine matter of difference, to haue a conuenient chosen number of the best learned of either part, & to confer togither their opinions and reasons, and therby to come to some good and charitable agreement.

1558/9: Parliament Passes the Act of Uniformity, Restoring the Protestant Rites of the Book of Common Prayer of Edward VI

Where at the death of our late sovereign lord King Edward VI there remained one uniform order of common service and prayer, and of the administration of sacraments, rites, and ceremonies in the Church of England, which was set forth in one book, intituled: The Book of Common Prayer, and Administration of Sacraments, and other rites and ceremonies in the Church of England; authorized by Act of Parliament holden in the fifth and sixth years of our said late sovereign lord King Edward VI, intituled: An Act for the uniformity of common prayer, and administration of the sacraments; the which was repealed and taken away by Act of Parliament in the first year of the reign of our late sovereign lady Queen Mary, to the great decay of the due honour of God, and discomfort to the professors of the truth of Christ's religion:

1559: Parliament Passes the Act of Supremacy Making the Queen (or King) Head of the Church and Requiring a Loyalty Oath from All Clergymen

And for the better observation and maintenance of this Act, may it please your highness that it may be further enacted by the authority aforesaid, that all and every archbishop, bishop, and all and every other ecclesiastical person, and other ecclesiastical officer and minister; of what estate, dignity, preeminence, or degree soever he or they be or shall be, and all and every temporal judge, justice, mayor, and other lay or temporal officer and minister, and every other person having your highness's fee or wages, within this realm, or any your highness's dominions, shall make, take, and receive a corporal oath upon the evangelist, before such person or persons as shall please your highness, your heirs or successors, under the great seal of England to assign and name, to accept and to take the same according to the tenor and effect hereafter following, that is to say:

I, A. B., do utterly testify and declare in my conscience, that the queen's highness is the only supreme governor of this realm, and of all other her highness's dominions and countries, as well in all spiritual or ecclesiastical things or causes, as temporal, and that no foreign prince, person, prelate, state or potentate, has, or ought to have, any jurisdiction, power, superiority, preeminence, or authority ecclesiastical or spiritual, within this realm; and therefore I do utterly renounce and forsake all foreign jurisdictions, powers, superiorities, and authorities, and do promise that from henceforth I shall bear faith and true allegiance to the queen's highness, her heirs and lawful successors, and to my power shall assist and defend all

jurisdictions, pre-eminences, privileges, and authorities granted or belonging to the queen's highness, her heirs and successors, or united and annexed to the imperial crown of this realm. So help me God, and by the contents of this book.

And that it may be also enacted, that if any such archbishop, bishop, or other ecclesiastical officer or minister, or any of the said temporal judges, justiciaries, or other lay officer or minister, shall peremptorily or obstinately refuse to take or receive the said oath, that then he so refusing shall forfeit and lose, only during his life, all and every ecclesiastical and spiritual promotion, benefice, and office, and every temporal and lay promotion and office, which he has solely at the time of such refusal made; and that the whole title, interest, and incumbency, in every such promotion, benefice, and other office, as against such person only so refusing, during his life, shall clearly cease and be void, as though the party so refusing were dead.

19. From Richard Hooker, the Preface to *The Laws of Ecclesiastical Polity* (1593)

Hooker, one of the principal architects of this via media, *argued for a wise balance between obedience to the inner stirrings of the individual conscience and obedience to the shepherds of the established church.*

In this passage he mediates between those positions. Hooker handles controversies that had already led to fiery martyrdoms and civil chaos. Nevertheless, in mild and generous tones he expresses profound doubts about the ability of "the common sort of men" to make public pronouncements about either religion or "civil polity." His words could be used not only to uphold established order but to warn against the dangers of rash "innovation" in speech or print—or on the public stage. ⌀

The first mean whereby nature teacheth men to judge good from evil, as well in laws as in other things, is the force of their own discretion. Hereunto therefore St. Paul referreth oftentimes his own speech, to be considered of by them that heard him. By what means so many of the people are trained unto the liking of that discipline. "I speak as to them which have understanding, judge ye what I say." Again afterward, "Judge in yourselves, is it comely that a woman pray uncovered?" The exercise of this kind of judgment our Saviour requireth in the Jews. In them of Berea the Scripture commendeth it. Finally, whatsoever we do, if our own secret judgment consent not unto it as fit and good to be done, the doing of it to us is sin, although the thing itself be allowable. St. Paul's rule therefore generally is, "Let every man in his own mind be fully persuaded of that thing which he either alloweth or doth."

Some things are so familiar and plain, that truth from falsehood, and good from evil, is most easily discerned in them, even by men of no deep capacity. And of that nature, for the most part, are things absolutely unto all men's salvation necessary, either to be held or denied, either to be done or avoided. For which cause St. Augustine acknowledgeth, that they are not only set down, but also plainly set down in Scripture; so that he which heareth or readeth may without any great difficulty understand. Other things also there are belonging (though in a lower degree of importance) unto the offices of Christian men: which, because they are more obscure, more intricate and hard to be judged of, therefore God hath appointed some to spend their whole time principally in the study of things divine, to the end that in these more doubtful cases their understanding might be a light to direct others. "If the understanding power or faculty of the soul be" (saith the grand physician) "like unto bodily sight, not of equal sharpness in all, what can be more convenient than that, even as the dark-sighted man is directed by the clear about things visible; so likewise in matters of deeper discourse the wise in heart do shew the simple where his way lieth?" In our doubtful cases of law, what man is there who seeth not how requisite it is that professors of skill in that faculty be our directors? So it is in all other kinds of knowledge.

And even in this kind likewise the Lord hath himself appointed, that "the priest's lips should preserve knowledge, and that other men should seek the truth at his mouth, because he is the messenger of the Lord of hosts." Gregory Nazianzen, offended at the people's too great presumption in controlling the judgment of them to whom in such cases they should have rather submitted their own, seeketh by earnest entreaty to stay them within their bounds: "Presume not ye that are sheep to make yourselves guides of them that should guide you; neither seek ye to overskip the fold which they about you have pitched. It sufficeth for your part, if ye can well frame yourselves to be ordered. Take not upon you to judge your judges, nor to make them subject to your laws who should be a law to you; for God is not a God of sedition and confusion, but of order and of peace."

But ye will say that if the guides of the people be blind, the common sort of men must not close up their own eyes and be led by the conduct of such: if the priest be "partial in the law," the flock must not therefore depart from the ways of sincere truth, and in simplicity yield to be followers of him for his place sake and office over them. Which thing, though in itself most true, is in your defence notwithstanding weak; because the matter wherein ye think that ye see, and imagine that your ways are sincere, is of far deeper consideration than any one amongst five hundred of you conceiveth. Let the vulgar sort amongst you know, that there is not the least branch of the cause wherein they are so resolute, but to the trial of it a great deal more appertaineth than their conceit doth reach unto. I write not this in disgrace of the simplest that way given, but I would gladly they knew the nature of that cause wherein they think themselves throughly instructed and are not; by means whereof they daily run themselves, without feeling their own hazard, upon the dint of the Apostle's sentence against "evil-speakers as touching things wherein they are ignorant."

If it be granted a thing unlawful for private men, not called unto public consultation, to dispute which is the best state of civil polity, (with a desire of bringing in some other kind, than that under which they already live, for of such disputes I take it his meaning was;) if it be a thing confessed, that of such questions they cannot determine without rashness, inasmuch as a great part of them consisteth in special circumstances, and for one kind as many reasons may be brought as for another; is there any reason in the world, why they should better judge what kind of regiment ecclesiastical is the fittest? For in the civil state more insight, and in those affairs more experience a great deal must needs be granted them, than in this they can possibly have. When they which write in defence of your discipline and commend it unto the Highest not in the least cunning manner, are forced notwithstanding to acknowledge, "that with whom the truth is they know not," they are not certain; what certainty or knowledge can the multitude have thereof?

Weigh what doth move the common sort so much to favour this innovation, and it shall soon appear unto you, that the force of particular reasons which for your several opinions are alleged is a thing whereof the multitude never did nor could so consider as to be therewith wholly carried; but certain general inducements are used to make saleable your cause in gross; and when once men have cast a fancy towards it, any slight declaration of specialties will serve to lead forward men's inclinable and prepared minds.

20. The Thirty-Nine Articles of the Church of England (1572) and the Lambeth Articles (1595)

As extract 18 (above) shows, the Elizabethan church sought a theological "middle way," a negotiation between the Catholic and the Protestant "confessions" or dispensations; the Thirty-Nine Articles of the Church of England established the basic tenets for post-Reformation believers. Some of the excerpted articles here assert the clear and basic differences from Catholic doctrine, particularly in the matter of salvation and the notion of transubstantiation. Most interesting for this game, however, is Article 17 (below) on predestination, where one can see an

attempt to mitigate the harshness of Calvinist doctrine and its severe limitation on the number of people allowed salvation. The predestination clause attempts to be much more hopeful about the possibilities of God's grace than many Protestant theologians allowed.

By way of contrast: although a few years past the date of the game, the Lambeth Articles, drawn up by William Whitaker, Regius Professor of Divinity in Cambridge, and accepted or adopted by Archbishop Whitgift to supplement the Thirty-Nine Articles, were a clear attempt to move toward a more restrictive Calvinist theology. The irony here is that Whitgift himself was a relentless persecutor of Puritans and their divines, whose doctrines of salvation the Lambeth Articles more closely resemble than do the Thirty-Nine Articles. But under the Act of Supremacy of 1559, Queen Elizabeth was supreme governor of the church, and she had no intention "of allowing her Church to be taken over by the Puritan element within it."[1] Because she had repeatedly supported Whitgift even in his most vicious anti-Puritan activities, he should not have been surprised that she would prevent the doctrinally radical Lambeth Articles from ever being formally adopted. ⅁

From the Thirty-Nine Articles of the Church of England

VI. OF THE SUFFICIENCIE OF THE HOLY SCRIPTURES FOR SALUATION.

Holye Scripture conteyneth all thinges necessarie to saluation: so that whatsoeuer is not read therein, nor may be proued therby, is not to be required of anye man, that it shoulde be beleued as an article of the fayth, or be thought requisite as necessarie to saluation.

In the name of holy Scripture, we do vnderstande those Canonicall bookes of the olde and newe Testament, of whose aucthoritie was neuer any doubt in the Churche.

1. Gerald M. Pinciss and Roger Lockyer, *Shakespeare's World: Background Readings in the English Renaissance*, (New York: Continuum, 1989), 46.

XI. OF THE IUSTIFICATION OF MAN.

We are accompted righteous before God, only for the merite of our Lord and sauiour Jesus Christe, by faith, and not for our owne workes or deseruynges. Wherefore, that we are justified by fayth onely, is a most wholesome doctrine, and very full of comfort, as more largely is expressed in the Homilie of iustification.

XII. OF GOOD WORKES.

Albeit that good workes, which are the fruites of fayth, and folowe after iustification, can not put away our sinnes, and endure the seueritie of Gods iudgement: yet are they pleasing and acceptable to God in Christe, and do spring out necessarily of a true and huely fayth, in so muche that by them, a lyuely fayth may be as euidently knowen, as a tree discerned by the fruit.

XVII. OF PREDESTINATION AND ELECTION.

Predestination to lyfe, is the euer-lastyng purpose of God, whereby (before the foundations of the world were layd) he hath constantly decreed by his councell secrete to vs, to deliver from curse and damnation, those whom he hath chosen in Christe out of mankynde, and to bryng them by Christe to euerlastyng saluation, as vessels made to honour. Wherefore they which be indued with so excellent a benefite of God, be called accordyng to Gods purpose by his spirite workyng in due season: they through grace obey the callyng: they be iustified freely: they be made sonnes of God by adoption: they be made lyke the image of his onelye begotten sonne Jesus Christe: they walke religiously in good workes, and at length by gods mercy, they attaine to euerlastyng felicitie.

As the godly consyderation of predestination, and our election in Christe, is full of sweete, pleasaunt, and vnspeakeable comfort to godly persons, and such as feele in them selues the working of the spirite of Christe, mortifying the workes of the fleshe, and their earthlye members, and drawing up their mynde to hygh and heauenly thinges, aswell because it doth greatly establyshe and confirme their fayth of eternal saluation to be enioyed through Christ, as because it doth feruently kindle their loue towardes God: So, for curious and carnal persons, lacking the spirite of Christe, to haue continually before their eyes the sentence of Gods predestination, is a most daungerous downefall, whereby the deuyll doth thrust them either into desperation, or into reckelesnesse of most vncleane living, no lesse perilous then desperation.

Furthermore, we must receaue Gods promises in such wyse, as they be generally set foorth to vs in holy scripture: and in our doynges, that wyl of God is to be folowed, which we haue expreslye declared vnto vs in the worde of God.

XXVIII. OF THE LORDES SUPPER.

The Supper of the Lord, is not only a signe of the love that Christians ought to haue among them selues one to another: but rather it is a Sacrament of our redemption by Christes death. Insomuch that to suche as ryghtlie, worthyly, and with fayth receaue the same the bread whiche we breake is a parttakyng of the body of Christe, and likewyse the cuppe of blessing, is a parttakyng of the blood of Christe.

Transubstantiation (or the chaunge of the substaunce of bread and wine) in the Supper of the Lorde, can not be proued by holye writ, but is repugnaunt to the playne wordes of scripture, ouerthroweth the nature of a Sacrament, and hath geuen occasion to many superstitions.

The body of Christe is geuen, taken, and eaten in the Supper only after an heauenly and spirituall maner: And the meane whereby the body of Christe is receaued and eaten in the Supper, is fayth.

The Sacrament of the Lordes Supper was not by Christes ordinaunce reserued, caryed about, lyfted up, or worshipped.

The Lambeth Articles (1595)

1. God from eternity has predestined some men to life, and reprobated some to death.
2. The moving or efficient cause of predestination to life is not the foreseeing of faith, or of perseverance, or of good works, or of anything innate in the person of the

predestined, but only the will of the good pleasure of God.

3. There is a determined and certain number of predestined, which cannot be increased or diminished.

4. Those not predestined to salvation are inevitably condemned on account of their sins.

5. A true, lively and justifying faith, and the sanctifying Spirit of God, is not lost nor does it pass away either totally or finally in the elect.

6. he truly faithful man—that is, one endowed with justifying faith—is sure by full assurance of faith ("plerophoria fidei") of the remission of sins and his eternal salvation through Christ.

7. Saving grace is not granted, is not made common, is not ceded to all men, by which they might be saved, if they wish.

8. No one can come to Christ unless it be granted to him, and unless the Father draws him: and all men are not drawn by the Father to come to the Son.

9. It is not in the will or power of each and every man to be saved.

21. The Continuing Catholic Threat: Pope Pius V Urges All English Catholics to Disobey the Queen (1570)

Of course the Elizabethan Settlement did not end Roman Catholicism in England, though by the end of Elizabeth's long reign the numbers of Catholics had dwindled. Even so, there were many Englishmen loyal to the old church, possibly including John Shakespeare, father of the playwright. The Roman church had long been linked with fears of foreign subversion, and these fears had some basis. In 1570 the pope issued the following declaration condemning the Queen, and the next pope encouraged loyal Catholics to assassinate her. This threat seemed all too real amid the terrors of religious violence in Europe. ℘

A Declaration (1570; an Early English Transcription):
Pius, bishop, seruant of Gods seruants, &c.
Shee (queene Elisabeth) hath cleane put awaie the sacrifice of the masse, praiers, fastings, choise or difference of meats & single life. Shee inuaded the kingdome, & by vsurping monstrouslie the place of the supreme head of the church in all England, and the cheefe authoritie & iurisdiction of the same, hath againe broght the said realme into miserable destruction. Shee hath remooued the noble men of England from the kings councell. She hath made her councell of poore, darke, beggerlie fellows, and hath placed them ouer the people. These councellors are not onlie poore & beggerlie, but also heretikes. Unto her all such as are the woorst of the people resort, and are by her receiued into safe protection, &c. We make it knowen, that Elisabeth aforesaid, & as manie as stand on her side in the matters abouenamed, haue run into the danger of our cursse. We make it also knowen, that we haue depriued her from that right shée pretended to haue in the kingdome aforesaid and also from all and euerie her authoritie, dignitie, and priuilege. We charge and forbid all and euerie the nobles, and subiects, and people, and others aforesaid, that they be not so hardie as to obeie her or her will, or commandements, or laws, vpon paine of the like accursse vpon them. We pronounce that all whosoeuer by anie occasion haue taken their oath vnto hir, are for euer discharged of such their oath, and also from all fealtie and seruice, which was due to her by reason of her gouernment, &c.

22. Tichborne's *Elegy*
In 1572, thousands of French Protestants were massacred on Saint Bartholomew's Day, a real-life horror story revived by Christopher Marlowe in The Massacre at Paris, a play for the London stage. Elizabeth felt herself besieged by Catholic plots that aimed to put her cousin Mary Stuart, Queen of Scots, on the English throne. Indeed, concern for the Queen's safety prompted the Privy Council to pass a Bond of Association (1584), condemning any heir to the throne who might benefit from a plot to remove Elizabeth, even if the heir were unaware of the plot! The bond also conscripted the nobility to avenge any such plot against the Queen.

In 1586, the Queen's spymaster, Sir Francis Walsingham, discovered (after conniving to encourage the conspirators) the so-called Babington Plot to assassinate Elizabeth and put Mary Stuart on the throne.

The conspirators in that plot were hanged, drawn, and quartered. One of the commissioners at the trial of the plotters was the Queen's trusted courtier, Sir Christopher Hatton, who somewhat hysterically or at least hyperbolically summed up the crown's argument about the extent of the treasons: ℘

First he showed how these wicked and devilish youths had conspired to murder the Queen's most excellent Majest; secondly, to bring in Foreign invasion; thirdly, to deliver the Queen of Scots and make her Queen; fourthly, to sack the City of London; fiftly, to rob and destroy all the wealthy subjects of this Realm; sixthly, to kill divers of the Privy Council . . . ; seventhly, to set fire on all the Queen's ships; eighthly, to cloy all the great ordnance; ninthly, and lastly, to subvert religion and the whole state of government. The inventors and beginners whereof were these devilish priests and seminaries . . . who now a days do not go about to seduce the ancient and discreet men . . . but they assail with their persuasions the younger sort, and of those the most ripe wits, whose high hearts and ambitious minds do carry them headlong to all wickedness. In the end he concluded with remorse for the youth of some of these unhappy men . . . and also shewed forth a notable proof of the falsehood of these lying Papists, which was a book printed at Rome, and made by the Papists, wherein they affirm, that the English Catholics, which suffer for religion, be lapped in bear-skins, and baited to death with dogs—a most monstrous lie and manifest falsehood.[1]

On the eve of his execution, one of the conspirators, Sir Chidiock Tichborne, wrote in a letter to his wife elegiac verses reflecting stoically on the ironies of his short life. The stylish stanzas were published soon after Tichborne's execution, along with patriotic verses

written in reply (possibly by the playwright Thomas Kyd). The pair of poems gives us a sense of the primacy of poetry as a method of making sense of experience, both private and public, in Elizabethan England. Tichborn's poem is void of political or religious reference, unlike the scornful and triumphant reply. ℘

My prime of youth is but a frost of cares,
My feast of joy is but a dish of pain,
My crop of corn is but a field of tares,[1]
And all my good is but vain hope of gain;
The day is past, and yet I saw no sun,
And now I live, and now my life is done.

My tale was heard and yet it was not told,
My fruit is fallen, and yet my leaves are green,
My youth is spent and yet I am not old,
I saw the world and yet I was not seen;
My thread is cut and yet it is not spun,
And now I live, and now my life is done.

I sought my death and found it in my womb,
I looked for life and saw it was a shade,
I trod the earth and knew it was my tomb,
And now I die, and now I was but made;
My glass is full, and now my glass is run,
And now I live, and now my life is done.

23. Hendecasyllabon T. K. in Cygneam Cantionem Chideochi Tychborne [Ten-Syllable Verses on the Swan Song of Chidiock Tichborne]

Thy prime of youth is frozen with thy faults,
Thy feast of joy is finisht with thy fall;
Thy crop of corn is tares availing naughts,
Thy good God knows thy hope, thy hap and all.
Short were thy days, and shadowed was thy sun,
T'obscure thy light unluckily begun.

Time trieth truth, and truth hath treason tripped;
Thy faith bare fruit as thou hadst faithless been:
Thy ill spent youth thine after years hath nipt;

---

1. Harris Nicholas, *The Life and Times of Sir Christopher Hatton* (London, 1847), 447–48.

1. *tares:* weeds

And God that saw thee hath preserved our Queen.
Her thread still holds, thine perished though unspun,
And she shall live when traitors lives are done.

Thou soughtst thy death, and found it in desert,
Thou look'dst for life, yet lewdly forc'd it fade:
Thou trodst the earth, and now on earth thou art,
As men may wish thou never hadst been made.
Thy glory, and thy glass[1] are timeless run;
And this, O Tychborne, hath thy treason done.

24. Queen Elizabeth to Sir Amyas Paulet, 1586

*The Babington Plot persuaded the Queen to place
Mary Stuart in stricter confinement, and soon after
try her for treason. The Queen's instructions to
Mary's jailer, Sir Amyas Paulet, vividly convey a
royal mix of gratitude and fear, fury and piety. ⚘*

Amyas, my most careful and faithful servant,
God reward thee treblefold in the double for thy
most troublesome charge so well discharged. If you
knew, my Amyas, how kindly, besides dutifully, my
careful heart accepts your double labors and
faithful actions, your wise orders and safe regards
performed in so dangerous and crafty a charge, it
would ease your troubles' travail and rejoice your
heart. In which I charge you to carry this most
nighest thought: that I cannot balance in any
weight of my judgment the value that I prize you at.
And suppose no treasure to countervail such a
faith, and condemn me in that behalf which I never
committed if I reward not such deserts. Yea, let me
lack when I have most need if I acknowledge not
such a merit with a reward *non omnibus datum*.[2]

But let your wicked mistress know how,
with hearty sorrow, her vile deserts compels these
orders; and bid her, from me, ask God forgiveness
for her treacherous dealing toward the saver of her
life many years, to the intolerable peril of her own.
And yet not content with so many forgivenesses,
must fall again so horribly, far passing a woman's

1. *glass:* hourglass
2. *non omnibus datum:* not given to all

thought, much more a princess, instead of excus-
ing, whereof not one can serve, it being so plainly
confessed by the actors of my guiltless death. Let
repentance take place; and let not the fiend possess
her so as her best part be lost, which I pray with hands
lifted up to Him that may both save and spill, with
my loving adieu and prayer for thy long life.

Your most assured and loving sovereign in
heart, by good desert induced, Elizabeth Regina.[1]

25. Queen Elizabeth I, Speech to the Troops at Tilbury

*Soon after Mary's execution, King Philip of Spain
(widower of Mary Tudor) organized an invasion
of England, partly because as a pious Catholic he
considered Elizabeth a heretic. In 1588, in the midst
of hostilities against Spain, she helped inspire the
troops who braced for an attack by the Spanish
Armada (their feared military sea power of Spain)
in Tilbury, Essex, by delivering this legendary speech,
a masterpiece of self-presentation and politic
promise. Note her skill at transforming weakness
into strength and controversy into certainty.*

*The destruction in 1588 of the Armada, less through
military action than a terrible storm at sea, was looked
on by English Protestants as an act of divine inter-
vention. Even so, some very important English families
(most famously the Howards, Dukes of Norfolk)
remained Roman Catholics throughout Elizabeth's
reign. Her closest advisers, including Burghley and
Robert Cecil, used the threat of Catholic uprising to
strengthen their own power and to manipulate the
aging queen's decisions, especially as she faced
death without an heir. ⚘*

My loving people,
We have been persuaded by some that are
careful of our safety, to take heed how we commit our selves to armed multitudes, for fear of
treachery; but I assure you I do not desire to live to
distrust my faithful and loving people. Let tyrants

1. *Regina*: Queen

fear, I have always so behaved myself that, under God, I have placed my chiefest strength and safeguard in the loyal hearts and good-will of my subjects; and therefore I am come amongst you, as you see, at this time, not for my recreation and disport, but being resolved, in the midst and heat of the battle, to live and die amongst you all; to lay down for my God, and for my kingdom, and my people, my honour and my blood, even in the dust. I know I have the body but of a weak and feeble woman; but I have the heart and stomach of a king, and of a king of England too, and think foul scorn that Parma or Spain, or any prince of Europe, should dare to invade the borders of my realm; to which rather than any dishonour shall grow by me, I myself will take up arms, I myself will be your general, judge, and rewarder of every one of your virtues in the field. I know already, for your forwardness you have deserved rewards and crowns; and we do assure you in the word of a prince, they shall be duly paid you. In the mean time, my lieutenant general[1] shall be in my stead, than whom never prince commanded a more noble or worthy subject; not doubting but by your obedience to my general, by your concord in the camp, and your valour in the field, we shall shortly have a famous victory over those enemies of my God, of my kingdom, and of my people.

Reprinted as *"Speech to the Troops at Tilbury,"* Luminarium: Anthology of English Literature *website, April 12, 2012,* *http://www.luminarium.org/renlit/tilbury.htm.*

26. The Puritan Threat: *An Admonition to the Parliament*, Attributed to John Field and Thomas Wilcox (1572)

The so-called Elizabethan Settlement of Religion incorporated certain elements of the Protestant Reformation in the English church: a break from papal authority, liturgy in English, the Bible in translation for all to read, a married clergy, an end to monastic institutions, communion "in both kinds"

(bread and wine) for all communicants, and an emphasis on preaching. At the same time, the Church of England incorporated certain Catholic traditions, including sacramental rituals and a hierarchical church governance by bishops and archbishops. On certain doctrinal questions, like the "real presence" of Christ's body in the bread of communion and the central controversy over salvation through good works or faith in divine grace, the English church took no firm stand, leaving individual believers and priests room for interpretation. This moderate stance served most English Christians well enough, but it alienated radical Protestants, many of whom had grown more radical during the Catholic restoration of Mary's reign.*

In 1572, An Admonition to the Parliament *was published anonymously. It upholds the purity of early Christian worship, and finds impurity in several practices of the Elizabethan church, including the selection of priests by a corrupt system of bishops and patronage, "popish" ceremonies, and the ritual and doctrine of the Book of Common Prayer. ✆*

May it therefore please your wisdoms to understand, we in England are so far off from having a church rightly reformed according to the prescript of God's word, that as yet we are not come to the outward face of the same. For to speak of that wherein all consent, and whereupon all writers accord: the outward marks whereby a true Christian church is known, are preaching of the word purely, ministering of the sacraments sincerely, and ecclesiastical discipline which consisteth in admonition and correction of faults severely. Touching the first, namely the ministry of the word, although it must be confessed that the substance of doctrine by many delivered is sound and good, yet herein it faileth, that neither the ministers thereof are according to God's word proved, elected, called, or ordained: nor the function in such sort so narrowly looked unto, as of right it ought and is of necessity required. For whereas in the old church a trial was had both of their ability to instruct and of their godly conversation also, now by the letters commendatory of some one man, noble or other, tag

---

1. Robert Dudley, Earl of Leicester; he was the Queen's favorite, once rumored to be her lover, later replaced in position and rumor by Robert Devereux, Earl of Essex.

and rag, learned and unlearned, of the basest sort of the people (to the slander of the Gospel in the mouths of the adversaries) are freely received. In those days no idolatrous sacrificers or heathenish priests were appointed to be preachers of the Gospel: but we allow and like well of popish mass-mangers, men for all seasons, King Henry's priests, King Edward's priests, Queen Mary's priests, who of a truth (if God's word were precisely followed) should from the same be utterly removed.

Then [in early Christian times] they taught others; now they must be instructed themselves, and therefore like young children they must be taught catechisms. Then election was made by the common consent of the whole church: now every one picketh out for himself some notable good benefice, he obtaineth the next advowson [= appointment to office] by money or by favor, and so thinketh himself to be sufficiently chosen. Then the congregation had authority to call ministers; instead thereof now they run, they ride, and by unlawful suit and buying, prevent other suitors also. Then no minister [was] placed in any congregation but by consent of the people; now that authority is given into the hands of the bishop alone, who by his sole authority thrusteth upon them such as they many times as well for unhonest life, as also for lack of learning, may and do justly dislike. Then none [was] admitted to the ministry, but a place was void beforehand to which he should be called; but now bishops (to whom the right of ordering ministers doth at no hand appertain) do make 60, 80, or a 100 at a clap, and send them abroad into the country like masterless men. Then after just trial and vocation they were admitted to their function, by laying on of the hands of the company of the eldership only; now there is (neither of these being looked unto) required [apparel, including] an alb, a surplice, a vestment, a pastoral staff, beside that ridiculous, and (as they use it to their new creatures) blasphemous saying, "Receive the holy ghost."

Then every pastor had his flock, and every flock his shepherd, or else shepherds; now they do not only run fisking [= scampering] from place to place [because one minister may be appointed to several churches or "livings"] (a miserable disorder in Gods church) but covetously join living to living, making shipwreck of their own consciences, and being but one shepherd (nay, would to God they were shepherds and not wolves) had many flocks. Then the ministers were preachers; now bare readers. And if any be so well disposed to preach in their own charges, they may not without my Lord's license. In those days known by voice, learning, and doctrine; now they must be discerned from other by popish and Antichristian apparel, as cap, gown, tippet, etc. Then, as God gave utterance they preached the word only; now they read homilies, articles, injunctions, etc.

Then it was painful; now gainful. Then poor and ignominious; now rich and glorious. And therefore titles, livings, and offices by Antichrist devised are given to them, as Metropolitan, Archbishop, Lord's Grace, Lord Bishop, Suffragan, Dean, Archdeacon, Prelate of the Garter, Earl, County Palatine, Honor, High Commissioners, Justices of Peace and Quorum, etc. All which, together with their offices, as they are strange and unheard of in Christ's church, nay plainly in God's word forbidden, so are they utterly with speed out of the same to be removed.

Then ministers were not tied to any form of prayer invented by man, but as the spirit moved them, so they poured forth hearty supplications to the Lord. Now they are bound of necessity to a prescript order of service and book of common prayer in which a great number of things contrary to God's word are contained, as baptism by women, private Communions, Jewish purifyings, observing of holy days, etc., patched (if not all together, yet the greatest piece) out of the Pope's portuis [= handbook]. Then feeding the flock diligently; now teaching quarterly. Then preaching in season; now once in a month is thought sufficient, if twice, it is judged a work of supererogation [= excess]. Then nothing taught but God's word; now princes' pleasures, men's devices, popish ceremonies, and Antichristian rites in public pulpits defended. Then they sought them; now they seek theirs.

27. Witchcraft and Demonology: From Henry Holland, *A Treatise against Witchcraft* (1590)

The topics of witchcraft, magic, and, more generally, demonology in the early modern period are extraordinarily fertile, as many contemporary tracts, trial testimonies, and sermons about the subject attest. One of the best-known of these discussions, Reginald Scot's A Discoverie of Witchcraft *(1584), takes a highly skeptical—some might say modern—view of the possibility that witches, such "poor, old women," could wield the power and destructiveness their alleged victims aver. (Viewed from another angle, as historian Diana Purkiss notes, Scot's disbelief carries nearly as much patriarchal presumption as does the routine misogyny of witch persecutors). Scot held that, while magic and conjuring were possible, they required training and education to accomplish. His view seemed like a rational corrective to witch hysteria, but it infuriated none other than Scotland's King James VI (later to be England's James I), who claimed not only personal knowledge of the existence of the dark arts but, later, victimhood as the target of hostile magical forces. Supposedly, a group of witches conjured a storm in 1590 to shipwreck and drown the King on his way to wed Anne of Denmark; he oversaw the trial of the unfortunate suspects himself, and not surprisingly won convictions. Later he wrote his own tract on the subject,* Daemonologie *(1597); when he ascended to the throne in England, he sought to burn all copies of Scot's tract.*

Henry Holland, a minister from a town near Cambridge, likewise responds to Scot's Discoverie—*repeatedly referred to in this excerpt parenthetically—with scorn and defensiveness. It seems that religious and political authorities found disbelief in witchcraft and demons nearly as dangerous as adherence to the evil forces themselves. Stuart Clark, an eminent historian of witchcraft (see his* Thinking with Demons *[1997]), notes that "at the heart of the crime [of witchcraft] was the demonic pact, but not so much for the feats which it subsequently enabled individuals to achieve, as for the act of apostasy itself—a kind of allegiance which Henry Holland . . . likened to treason and rebellion against* 'the kingdome and Citie of God.'*"[1] Such rebellions were almost always what authority feared most.* ✆

A Treatise against witchcraft:

Or, A dialogue wherein the greatest doubts concerning that sinne are briefly answered: a Sathanicall operation in the witchcraft of all times is truly prooved: the most precious preservatives against such evils are shewed: very needful to be knowen of all men, but chiefly of the Masters and Fathers of families, that they may learn the best way to purge their houses of all unclean spirits, and wisely to avoide the dreadfull impieties and greate daungers which come by such abhominations.

TO THE RIGHT HONOVRABLE LORD Robert Deveraux, Earle of Essex and EWE, Vicount of Hereford and Bourchier, Lord Ferrers of Chartley, Bourchier and Lovaine, Master of the Queenes Maiesties Horse, and Knight of the most Honourable order of the Garter. H. H. wisheth with his heart, grace from God the Father by Iesus Christ, increase of al vertues, and con|stancie in the truth of the Gospell to the ende.

THE Scriptures of God (right Honourable) in sundrie places, doe most euidently teach vs, that there are two spirituall kingdomes in this world, which haue continual hatred & bloody wars, without hope of truce for euer. The Lord and king of the one, is our Lord Iesus, the tyrannical vsurper of the other, is Sathan, Again, this also we are as clearely taught, that all men liuing without exception, are eyther true subiects of the one, or slaues vnto the other. For albeit, the Neuters of this worlde, dreame that they may indifferentlie view the scarres and woundes of other men, and neuer approch neere those bloody skirmishes: yet the truth is, they are fowlie deceiued: for the great Lord and King

---

1. Stuart Clark, "Sin, Superstition, and Society (c. 1520–1620)," in *New Perspectives on Witchcraft, Magic, and Demonology*, vol. 1, ed. Brian P. Levack (New York: Routledge, 2001), 192.

hath said with his owne mouth, [Note: Matt. 12:30] Hee that is not with mee, is against mee. Wherefore, all that build not vp, as much as in them lyeth, the kingdome and Citie of God, and batter downe the holdes of Sathan, must be numbred with the rebels and enemies of our Lord Christ, when the warrefare shalbe ended. The enemies of Christ haue euer beene many, some open, cruell, foes without: some subtill, close conspirators within the house of God, most daungerous vnderminers of the Citie of God, if they be not discouered. In this secret conspiracie, albeit Sathan haue many Champions, and many artes, mille artes, mille nocendi modos: there is no arte more effectuall and dreadfull in my iudgement, then those his wicked faculties in Witchcrafte. I haue indeauoured (right Honourable) in this small Treatise, according to my poore strength, to shewe the principall meanes ordained of God for to confound and to discouer them. I doe here therefore humbly aske your Honourable protection, for the defence of the trueth and the glory of God, against all the patrones of all such vile artes, and horrible abhominations. Thus doeing, your Honour shall not onely encourage me, but also, imbolden others, which are better able, and wil be willing also, to lay open the secret delusions and practises of Sathans inventions. Nobilitie without godlines and vertue (as your Honour well knoweth) is blood indeede, as a learned man speaketh, but blood without bones and sinewes. I knowe therefore that to increase in your Honour true Nobilitie, you are well assured, that it principally standeth in purchasing vnto Christ and his Church, true honour and glorie, and in beating downe (as much as in your Honour lyeth) all the holdes of Sathans kingdome. God increase in your heart (right Honourable) all his good graces to his glory, your own saluation, and the benefit of his Church. Amen. The yeere of our saluation. 1590.

Your good Lordships euer to vse and command in the Lord, Henr. Holland.

[From the dialogue between Theophilus, "lover of God," and Mysodaemon, "unclean demon":]

THEOPHILUS.
I will not be long in the confirmation of these pointes, for that other writers haue written much of this matter. First, for the witches bargaine and obligation with the deuill, [Note: The witches bargaine with the deuill] answer me a few questions, Mysodaemon: are you resolued that there were euer any witches in the world?

MYSODAEMON.
That I am, those mentioned in the Scripture: and peraduenture some other beside.

THEOPHILUS.
And canst thou imagine that Sathan would binde him selfe to any of them (as the witch of Endor for example) to be present when they would, and to minister vnto their necessities, as we read he did, before such time as the witch also for her part doe renounce God & all religion, [Note: 1 Sam. 28] & adore him as her God: yea and binde her selfe in some euident manner, to persist in this profession, and continually to performe these pointes, and all other articles conteined in his obligation.

MYSODAEMON.
If there be such a bargaine, the deuil, no doubt, wilbe sure enough for his part: and I think he wil not greatly bind him selfe before the witch also doe the same.

THEOPHILUS.
It is most like to be true, Mysodaemon, for sometimes there obligations are found written with their own blood, as Bodin[1] reporteth of one, Theophilus, to haue done.

1. Jean Bodin (1530-96), economist and political scientist, author of a volume on witchcraft, *De la Démonomanie des Sorciers* (1587).

MYSODAEMON.

I will not heare, I tell you, neither of Bodins bables, nor Sprengeus fables: I pray you shew me one example out of some credible Authour, if you can.

THEOPHILUS.

Master Fox [John Foxe wrote the *Book of Martyrs*, 1565] in the storie of M. Luther, hath one singular example for this purpose. There was (saith he) a young man about Wittemberge, who beeing kept bare and needie by his father, was tempted by way of sorcerie, to bargaine with the Deuill, or a familiar (as they call him) to yeeld him selfe bodie and soule into the deuils power, vpon condition to haue his wish satisfied with money: so that vpon the same, an obligation was made by the young man, written with his owne blood, and giuen to the deuill. This case you see how horrible it was, and how damnable: now heare what followed. Vpon this sodaine wealth and alteration of this young man, the matter first beeing noted, began afterwaerdes more and more to be suspected, and at length after long & great admiration, was brought to M. Luther to be examined. The young man whether for shame or feare long denied to confesse, and would be knowen of nothing. Yet God so wrought beeing stronger then the deuill, that be vttered vnto Luther the whole substance of the case, as well touching the money as the obligation, Luther vnderstanding the matter, and pittying the lamentable state of the man, willed the whole congregation to pray: and he himselfe ceased not with prayers to labour, so that the deuill was compelled at the last to throw in his obligation at the window, and bad him take it againe vnto him. Thus farre Master Luther.

MYSODAEMON.

Surely this is a not able example: and it may be this is not so incredible a matter, as some haue marueilous boldly and confidently auouched: but where make they such bargaines?

THEOPHILUS.

At their common meetings, which they cal their sabboth, for there the deuill hath many witnesses, and there these obligations are autentically sealed. For thou must vnderstande, Misodaemon, that as thou knowest Sathans purpose is euer most to rebell against God: so his drift in all the artes of magike principallie is, to vse all the mockerie that euer he can inuent against God, and his Word and all the partes of true religion. And to this end, he hath ordained his sabbothes for his seruice. In these horrible meetings, Sathan himselfe appeares sometime in one forme, sometime in another: (for so he can as the Scripture [Note: 2 Cor. 11:14] testifieth) for somtimes his ministers behould him in the likenes of a man, but most com|monly of a foule stinking goate. There they haue sundrie suites vnto him: and hee ministreth and teacheth them to confect poysons and pouders, and many things for the destruction of man and beast, and in the end he addeth (when his congregation is to be dismissed) with a terrible thundring voice, this speech, or something to the like effect. Vlciscimini vos, aut mortem oppetetis. Revenge your selues, or else die the death.

MYSODAEMON.

Well, Theophilus, these things may be true, yet some haue doubted how there can be any firme bargaine betweene a carnall bodie and a spirituall.

THEOPHILUS.

The Scripture telleth vs plainely that he can transforme him selfe into many shapes; the Apostle saith, he can change himselfe into an [Note: 2 Cor. 11:14] angell of light. . . .

MYSODAEMON.

What manifest and cleare testimonies of Scripture haue you against this practise?

THEOPHILUS.

There is nothing cleare and manifest, Mysodaemon, vnto those in whome the word of God abideth not, and which haue not ouercome that wicked one, which is the deuill: for Sathan so amazeth them, that they are more ready to reele into euery sinne, though it be neuer so monstrous, then to see the greatest light that God offereth them. Are not those prohibitions of God in his Law and in his Prophets so plaine and so evident, that (as the Prophet saith) he that runneth, may reade and vnderstand them? the Law of God is this, [Note: Lev. 19:31, 20:6; Deut. 18:10, 18:15] You shall not regard them that worke with spirits, neither soothsayers, yea shal not seeke them to be defiled by them, I am the Lord the God. Againe, anon after, to make the greatnes of this sinne the better to appeare, he repeateth the same wordes in more fearefull manner: If any turne after such as worke with spirites, and after soothsayers to goe a whoaring after them, then will I set my face against, that person, and will cut him of from his people. And againe, that God people might be sufficiently warned, they haue a third charge against this sinne in Deut. 18. where they are commaunded in all there necessities to seeke vnto God, and the ministerie of his worde: which place Es. commendeth to the Church of his time, on this manner: VVhen they shall say vnto you, enquire at them that haue a spirite of diuination, and at the soothsaiers which whisper and murmur, should not a people enquire at their God? from the liuing to the dead? to the law and to the testimonie, if they speake not according to this worde, it is because there is no light in them. And thus, Mysodaemon, the Lord hath most louingly warned, and most sharply charged his people to auoyde this sinne.

28. A Pragmatic Approach to Worldly Order: Machiavelli, *The Prince* (1515)

In Elizabethan England, Nicolo Machiavelli's The Prince *(not published in English translation until 1640) was known mainly by its scandalous reputation for godless, calculating cruelty. Some critics have read its recommendations as ironic or satirical, others as pragmatic, even scientific. Here follow two of the most controversial suggestions, concerning the use of fear and the practice of deception, both to preserve the good order of a princely state. ⌗*

From Chapter 17: Concerning Cruelty and Clemency, and Whether It Is Better to Be Loved than Feared

Upon this a question arises: whether it be better to be loved than feared or feared than loved? It may be answered that one should wish to be both, but, because it is difficult to unite them in one person, is much safer to be feared than loved, when, of the two, either must be dispensed with. Because this is to be asserted in general of men, that they are ungrateful, fickle, false, cowardly, covetous, and as long as you succeed they are yours entirely; they will offer you their blood, property, life and children, as is said above, when the need is far distant; but when it approaches they turn against you. And that prince who, relying entirely on their promises, has neglected other precautions, is ruined; because friendships that are obtained by payments, and not by greatness or nobility of mind, may indeed be earned, but they are not secured, and in time of need cannot be relied upon; and men have less scruple in offending one who is beloved than one who is feared, for love is preserved by the link of obligation which, owing to the baseness of men, is broken at every opportunity for their advantage; but fear preserves you by a dread of punishment which never fails.

Nevertheless a prince ought to inspire fear in such a way that, if he does not win love, he avoids hatred; because he can endure very well being feared whilst he is not hated, which will always be as long as he abstains from the property of his citizens and subjects and from their women. But when it is necessary for him to proceed against the life of someone, he must do it on proper justification and for manifest cause, but above all things he must keep his hands off the property of others, because men more quickly forget the death of their father than the loss of their patrimony. Besides, pretexts for taking away the property are never wanting; for he who has once begun to live by robbery will always find pretexts for seizing what belongs to others; but reasons for taking life, on the contrary, are more difficult to find and sooner lapse. But when a prince is with his army, and has under control a multitude of soldiers, then it is quite necessary for him to disregard the reputation of cruelty, for without it he would never hold his army united or disposed to its duties.

Among the wonderful deeds of Hannibal this one is enumerated: that having led an enormous army, composed of many various races of men, to fight in foreign lands, no dissensions arose either among them or against the prince, whether in his bad or in his good fortune. This arose from nothing else than his inhuman cruelty, which, with his boundless valour, made him revered and terrible in the sight of his soldiers, but without that cruelty, his other virtues were not sufficient to produce this effect. And shortsighted writers admire his deeds from one point of view and from another condemn the principal cause of them. That it is true his other virtues would not have been sufficient for him may be proved by the case of Scipio, that most excellent man, not of his own times but within the memory of man, against whom, nevertheless, his army rebelled in Spain; this arose from nothing but his too great forbearance, which gave his soldiers more licence than is consistent with military discipline. For this he was upbraided in the Senate by Fabius Maximus, and called the corrupter of the Roman soldiery. The Locrians were laid waste by a legate of Scipio, yet they were not avenged by him, nor was the insolence of the legate punished, owing entirely to his easy nature. Insomuch that someone in the Senate, wishing to excuse him, said there were many men who knew much better how not to err than to correct the errors of others. This disposition, if he had been continued in the command, would have destroyed in time the fame and glory of Scipio; but, he being under the control of the

Senate, this injurious characteristic not only concealed itself, but contributed to his glory.

Returning to the question of being feared or loved, I come to the conclusion that, men loving according to their own will and fearing according to that of the prince, a wise prince should establish himself on that which is in his own control and not in that of others; he must endeavour only to avoid hatred, as is noted.

From Chapter 18: Concerning the Way in Which Princes Should Keep Faith [i.e., Keep Their Word]

Every one admits how praiseworthy it is in a prince to keep faith, and to live with integrity and not with craft. Nevertheless our experience has been that those princes who have done great things have held good faith of little account, and have known how to circumvent the intellect of men by craft, and in the end have overcome those who have relied on their word. You must know there are two ways of contesting, the one by the law, the other by force; the first method is proper to men, the second to beasts; but because the first is frequently not sufficient, it is necessary to have recourse to the second. Therefore it is necessary for a prince to understand how to avail himself of the beast and the man. This has been figuratively taught to princes by ancient writers, who describe how Achilles and many other princes of old were given to the Centaur Chiron to nurse, who brought them up in his discipline; which means solely that, as they had for a teacher one who was half beast and half man, so it is necessary for a prince to know how to make use of both natures, and that one without the other is not durable. A prince, therefore, being compelled knowingly to adopt the beast, ought to choose the fox and the lion; because the lion cannot defend himself against snares and the fox cannot defend himself against wolves. Therefore, it is necessary to be a fox to discover the snares and a lion to terrify the wolves. Those who rely simply on the lion do not understand what they are about. Therefore a wise lord cannot, nor ought he to, keep faith when such observance may be turned against him, and when the reasons that caused him to pledge it exist no longer. If men were entirely good this precept would not hold, but because they are bad, and will not keep faith with you, you too are not bound to observe it with them. Nor will there ever be wanting to a prince legitimate reasons to excuse this nonobservance. Of this endless modern examples could be given, showing how many treaties and engagements have been made void and of no effect through the faithlessness of princes; and he who has known best how to employ the fox has succeeded best.

But it is necessary to know well how to disguise this characteristic, and to be a great pretender and dissembler; and men are so simple, and so subject to present necessities, that he who seeks to deceive will always find someone who will allow himself to be deceived. One recent example I cannot pass over in silence. Alexander VI did nothing else but deceive men, nor ever thought of doing otherwise, and he always found victims; for there never was a man who had greater power in asserting, or who with greater oaths would affirm a thing, yet would observe it less; nevertheless his deceits always succeeded according to his wishes, because he well understood this side of mankind.

Therefore it is unnecessary for a prince to have all the good qualities I have enumerated, but it is very necessary to appear to have them. And I shall dare to say this also, that to have them and always to observe them is injurious, and that to appear to have them is useful; to appear merciful, faithful, humane, religious, upright, and to be so, but with a mind so framed that should you require not to be so, you may be able and know how to change to the opposite.

And you have to understand this, that a prince, especially a new one, cannot observe all those things for which men are esteemed, being often forced, in order to maintain the state, to act contrary to faith, friendship, humanity, and religion. Therefore it is necessary for him to have a mind ready to turn itself accordingly as the winds and variations of fortune force it, yet, as I have said above, not to diverge from the good if he can avoid

doing so, but, if compelled, then to know how to set about it.

For this reason a prince ought to take care that he never lets anything slip from his lips that is not replete with the above-named five qualities, that he may appear to him who sees and hears him altogether merciful, faithful, humane, upright, and religious. There is nothing more necessary to appear to have than this last quality, inasmuch as men judge generally more by the eye than by the hand, because it belongs to everybody to see you, to few to come in touch with you. Every one sees what you appear to be, few really know what you are, and those few dare not oppose themselves to the opinion of the many, who have the majesty of the state to defend them; and in the actions of all men, and especially of princes, which it is not prudent to challenge, one judges by the result.

For that reason, let a prince have the credit of conquering and holding his state, the means will always be considered honest, and he will be praised by everybody because the vulgar are always taken by what a thing seems to be and by what comes of it; and in the world there are only the vulgar, for the few find a place there only when the many have no ground to rest on.

One prince [Maximilian, the Holy Roman emperor] of the present time, whom it is not well to name, never preaches anything else but peace and good faith, and to both he is most hostile, and either, if he had kept it, would have deprived him of reputation and kingdom many a time.

Nicolo Machiavelli (1469–1527), from The Prince, translated by W. K. Marriott (1908)

29. Marlowe's Machiavelli: The Prologue to *The Jew of Malta* (1591?)

Marlowe emphasizes the scheming, violent, and cynical qualities ascribed to Machiavelli by popular understanding. Note, however, the optimistic sense of self-creation, a certain unapologetic strutting, the respect for knowledge and intelligence as means to power, and the gleeful recognition of hypocrisy in his detractors. ℘

MACHEVILL speaks:

Albeit the world think Machevill is dead,
Yet was his soul but flown beyond the Alps,
And now the Guise[1] is dead, is come from France
To view this land, and frolic with his friends.
To some perhaps my name is odious,
But such as love me, guard me from their tongues,
And let them know that I am Machevill,
And weigh not men, and therefore not men's words:
Admired I am of those that hate me most.
Though some speak openly against my books,
Yet will they read me, and thereby attain
To Peter's chair:[2] and when they cast me off,
Are poisoned by my climbing followers.
I count religion but a childish toy,
And hold there is no sin but ignorance.
Birds of the air will tell of murders past?
I am ashamed to hear such fooleries:

Many will talk of title to a crown.
What right had Caesar to the Empire?
Might first made kings, and laws were then most sure
When like the Draco's[1] they were writ in blood.
Hence comes it, that a strong built citadel
Commands much more than letters can import:
Which maxima had Phalaris[2] observed,
H'had never bellowed in a brazen bull
Of great ones' envy; o'th' poor petty wites,[3]
Let me be envied and not pitied!
But whither am I bound, I come not, I,
To read a lecture here in Britaine,
But to present the tragedy of a Jew,
Who smiles to see how full his bags are crammed,
Which money was not got without my means.
I crave but this, grace him as he deserves,
And let him not be entertained the worse
Because he favours me.

---

1. **Guise:** The Duke of Guise, who led the massacre of French Protestants on Saint Bartholomew's Day, 1572. He would have seemed an archvillain to most Englishmen.

2. **Peter's chair:** The papacy, for which ambitious churchmen schemed and vied.

1. **Draco:** An Athenian lawmaker of proverbial, fear-inspiring severity; cf. *draconian*.

2. **Phalaris:** A Sicilian tyrant who roasted his enemies in a brass bull, and then was burned in it himself. Some writers say Phalaris was a scholar, so Machevill here claims his interest in "letters" led to his overthrow.

3. wites: either "wights" (creatures) or "wits"

Appendix: Maxims, Proverbs, *Sententiae, Adagia*

It was not uncommon for nobles and educated men and women to collect well-turned phrases in "sentence books," or compilations of wisdom and apt commentary on the human condition. Writing and speech in the early modern period were rife with such sentences (sententiae), or adages (adagia). The ability to quote or deploy these and other utterances was considered a sign of learning or at least rhetorical deftness. For an encyclopedic compendium of such phrases, see Morris P. Tilley, *A Dictionary of Proverbs in England in the Sixteenth and Seventeenth Centuries* (Ann Arbor: University of Michigan Press, 1950).

This brief collection may help ornament and illustrate your arguments and speeches; they may also impress your listeners, if the statements are well and judiciously used.

Many English versions of proverbs were directly translated and have become part of the common tongue. *The Adagia* (ca. 1500) of Erasmus contains familiar metaphors and turns of phrase that are now highly familiar. What we consider proverbs, or pearls of wisdom, appear often brilliantly in the work of the great French essayist Michel de Montaigne, whose skeptical *Essays* (ca. 1580) would come to have an immense influence on Shakespeare. Montaigne provided a rich fount of repeatable and terse learning and observations (as well as longer and complex meditations). Finally, a highly popular book in this vein is by John Bodenham, *Belvedere; or, The Garden of the Muses* (London, 1600).

FROM ERASMUS, *ADAGIA*
- Make haste slowly
- Take one step at a time
- He has one foot in Charon's boat [To have one foot in the grave]
- I gave as good as I got
- To call a spade a spade
- You are up to both ears [Up to your eyeballs]

- What's done cannot be undone
- We cannot all do everything
- Many hands make light work
- Where there's life, there's hope
- To cut to the quick
- Time reveals all things
- You shed crocodile tears
- You have touched the issue with a needle-point [You have gotten it exactly]
- Time tempers grief [Time heals all wounds]
- The dog is worthy of his dinner
- In the land of the blind, the one-eyed man is king
- No sooner said than done
- Between a stone and a shrine [Between a rock and a hard place]
- Like teaching an old man a new language [Can't teach an old dog new tricks]
- There's many a slip 'twixt cup and lip
- To squeeze water out of a stone
- To leave no stone unturned
- God helps those who help themselves
- The grass is greener over the fence
- To put the cart before the horse
- Dog in the manger
- One swallow [= bird] does not a summer make
- To break the ice
- Ship-shape
- To have an iron in the fire
- To look a gift horse in the mouth
- Neither fish nor flesh
- Like father, like son

MONTAIGNE, FROM THE *ESSAYS*
- Man in sooth is a marvellous, vain, fickle, and unstable subject.
- All passions that suffer themselves to be relished and digested are but moderate.
- It is not without good reason said, that he who

has not a good memory should never take upon him the trade of lying.

- The laws of conscience, which we pretend to be derived from nature, proceed from custom.
- There are some defeats more triumphant than victories.
- Nothing is so firmly believed as what we least know.
- The middle sort of historians (of which the most part are) spoil all; they will chew our meat for us.
- For a desperate disease a desperate cure.
- Plato says, "'Tis to no purpose for a sober man to knock at the door of the Muses;" and Aristotle says "that no excellent soul is exempt from a mixture of folly."
- A wise man never loses anything, if he has himself.
- I have here only made a nosegay of culled flowers, and have brought nothing of my own but the thread that ties them together.
- Men are most apt to believe what they least understand.
- I have never seen a greater monster or miracle in the world than myself.
- We seek and offer ourselves to be gulled.
- A little folly is desirable in him that will not be guilty of stupidity.
- There is no man so good, who, were he to submit all his thoughts and actions to the laws, would not deserve hanging ten times in his life.
- My appetite comes to me while eating.
- The oldest and best known evil was ever more supportable than one that was new and untried.
- I moreover affirm that our wisdom itself, and wisest consultations, for the most part commit themselves to the conduct of chance.
- We are born to inquire after truth; it belongs to a greater power to possess it. It is not, as Democritus said, hid in the bottom of the deeps, but rather elevated to an infinite height in the divine knowledge.
- It happens as with cages: the birds without despair to get in, and those within despair of getting out.
- Few men have been admired by their own domestics. [No man is a hero to his valet.]
- I speak truth, not so much as I would, but as much as I dare; and I dare a little the more as I grow older.
- The public weal requires that men should betray and lie and massacre.
- Nature forms us for ourselves, not for others; to be, not to seem.
- I find that the best virtue I have has in it some tincture of vice.
- One may be humble out of pride.
- How many worthy men have we seen survive their own reputation!
- Arts and sciences are not cast in a mould, but are formed and perfected by degrees, by often handling and polishing, as bears leisurely lick their cubs into form.
- Man is certainly stark mad; he cannot make a worm, and yet he will be making gods by the dozens.
- Some impose upon the world that they believe that which they do not; others, more in number, make themselves believe that they believe, not being able to penetrate into what it is to believe.
- Let us a little permit Nature to take her own way; she better understands her own affairs than we.
- For truth itself has not the privilege to be spoken at all times and in all sorts.

FROM JOHN BODENHAM, *BELVEDERE; OR, THE GARDEN OF THE MUSES*

- God will control when mortal men have done.
- Heaven works our fall, but yet the fault is ours.
- In vain do men contend against the stars.

- When hope and hap, when health and wealth is highest, / Then woe and wrack, disease and need is nighest.
- They love indeed that dare not say they love.
- To play the fool well is good sign of wit.
- Divided kingdoms make divided hearts.
- Kingdoms are fortune's fatal tennis balls.
- Law with extremity is extreme wrong.
- All men to some peculiar vice incline.
- Man is but mere calamity itself.
- What cannot women do that know their power?
- Death is far sweeter than the fear of death.
- Whiles timorous knowledge stands considering, / Audacious ignorance performs the deed.
- Fortune oft hurts when most she seems to help.
- A chance may win what by mischance was lost.
- It lies not in our power to love or hate, / For will in us is overruled by fate.
- Too much preciseness savors of self-love.
- We see the good but yet we choose the ill.
- Nothing is evil that is necessary.
- To die is all as common as to live.
- Near death he stands that stands too near a crown.

CPSIA information can be obtained
at www.ICGtesting.com
Printed in the USA
LVHW05s1327290818
588505LV00022B/652/P